D1715124

In Praise of Blood Sports
and Other Essays

WALTER SULLIVAN

In Praise of Blood Sports

and Other Essays

LOUISIANA STATE UNIVERSITY PRESS
Baton Rouge and London

Copyright © 1990 by Louisiana State University Press
All rights reserved
Manufactured in the United States of America
First printing
99 98 97 96 95 94 93 92 91 90   5 4 3 2 1

Designer: Laura Roubique Gleason
Typeface: Trump Mediaeval
Typesetter: The Composing Room of Michigan, Inc.
Printer and binder: Thomson-Shore, Inc.

LIBRARY OF CONGRESS CATALOGING-IN-PUBLICATION DATA

Sullivan, Walter, 1924–
    "In praise of blood sports" and other essays / Walter Sullivan.
       p. cm.
    ISBN 0–8071–1585–1 (alk. paper)
       1. American literature—Southern States—History and criticism.
    2. English fiction—20th century—History and criticism.
    3. Southern States in literature.   I. Title.
    PS261.S8 1990
    810.9'975—dc20   89–77831
                                                                   CIP

The author thanks the editor of the *Southern Literary Journal* for
permission to reprint "Richard Weaver and the Bishop's Widow," which
first appeared in a somewhat different form in the Spring, 1988, issue of
that journal. "The Two Worlds of William Golding" first appeared in the
July, 1987, issue of *The World and I* and is reprinted with permission from
The World and I, a publication of the Washington Times Corporation,
copyright © 1988. "Southern Writers in Spiritual Exile" is reprinted, with
permission, from *The "Southern Review" and Modern Literature, 1935–
1985*, edited by Lewis P. Simpson, James Olney, and Jo Gulledge, copyright
© 1988 by Louisiana State University Press.
    "Irony and Disorder: *The Secret Agent*," "A Sense of Place: Elizabeth
Bowen and the Landscape of the Heart," "Waugh Revisited," and "The
Last Agrarian: Peter Taylor Early and Late" were first published in the
Sewanee Review. Copyright 1973, 1976, 1984, and 1987 by the University
of the South. Reprinted by permission of the editor.

For
Jack Aden and Hal Weatherby
my colleagues in many losing battles

and for
George Core

Contents

Preface

Except for the essays on Joseph Conrad, Elizabeth Bowen, and Allen Tate, the pieces in this volume were written in the 1980s, most of them within the last two or three years. Except for "In Praise of Blood Sports," which appears here for the first time, all of them have been revised since their original publication—some extensively. I appreciate the opportunity the Louisiana State University Press has given me to offer these new versions; I hope they are improvements over the originals.

Since this is the third book I have published with the LSU Press, listing the people to whom I am indebted is almost a matter of designating the usual suspects. Beverly Jarrett urged me to submit these essays, and she shepherded the manuscript through the press committee. I am grateful to her, as I have had ample reason to be in the past, for her help and patience. I am grateful too to Marie Carmichael, who has been my editor in this project, and to Les Phillabaum, director of the press, for his kindness and generosity to me throughout our relationship and particularly now. Alberta Martin prepared the manuscript with the skill and intelligence usual in her work but hard to find elsewhere. Finally, wives of writers suffer their own grim lot in life, and my wife is, I am sorry to say, no exception. Jane has endured my silence and fits of preoccupation with scant complaint. I thank her for her forbearance and for the countless blessings she has brought to my life.

Part I

The Fathers and the Failures of Tradition

It is impossible, at this late date, to write of *The Fathers* without treading on ground that has already been covered. The novel has been part of Allen Tate's distinguished canon for more than half a century, and during that time it has received acute, if not extensive, critical analysis. One thinks immediately of Arthur Mizener's essay, but at one time or another most of us who have commented at all on Tate's work have touched on *The Fathers*; all are in general agreement concerning its basic delineations. Pleasant Hill is an image of southern society, a microcosm of a rigidly structured civilization, agrarian in nature, tainted by slavery, and operated under the terms of a highly developed social and moral code. Major Buchan is the patriarch of Pleasant Hill. Around and beneath him, his family and kin, his friends and chattels occupy stations to which they were born and according to which they assume privilege and responsibility to varying degrees. Thus Tate sketches the traditional southern civilization; against this he sets George Posey, who is in all of his dimensions a modern man. He is a product of the city, and because of this he suffers a fragmentation of intelligence and sensibility. Unlike Major Buchan, he is not part of a community—that construct so absolutely essential to the whole concept of southern culture—and, therefore, again unlike the major, he operates within a personal or private orientation. Major Buchan is by training and temperament unable to distinguish between his own and his family's welfare, and the felicity of his neighborhood and his nation. The two characters, representing opposing historical and cultural forces, come together in the opening pages of the book. The conflict is joined, and Major Buchan is found to be helpless against Posey. In this scene the story is given basic direction, and the beginning adumbrates the catastrophic end.

Major Buchan's ineffectualness in his confrontation with Posey is a major theme of southern literature. The traditional southern aristocrat, whose very southernness exists in the code by which he lives, is unable to defend that code against representatives of modernity who refuse to recognize or abide by the established ways. He must submit to defeat by the more pragmatic and therefore superior weapons of his adversary; or by fighting fire with fire, he loses anyway by ceasing to be what he was and therefore abandoning what he was struggling to preserve. In these terms we can explain most of the action of *The Fathers*. Tate reinforces our interpretation by allowing the ghost of Lacy Buchan's grandfather to tell the story of Jason and the Golden Fleece. This appeal to mythology is consonant with the particular kind of elegance that the book achieves—it is a poet's novel, juxtaposing as it does images of clarity against other images of mysterious density and employing language that ranges from simple to baroque. But my concern is with Posey, and to compare him with Jason is not to deliver him from that category of crass opportunists wherein are found such less presentable figures as Jason Compson and Flem Snopes. Posey prevails. Major Buchan achieves his final dignity in suicide. Pleasant Hill is reduced to ashes. The very last paragraph of the novel shows Lacy Buchan in the throes of that familiar ambiguity of spirit that he shares with a dozen other young southern heroes: think of Miranda at the end of "Old Mortality," or the narrator of Robert Penn Warren's "Blackberry Winter," or Quentin Compson's claim that he does not hate the South.

It is easy to see that the novel, in its broad configurations, resides in the fictional mainstream of the Southern Renascence, and in terms of its fundamental achievement it requires no further gloss from me. Therefore I want to address myself to two questions, one general and the other specific. First, why must the traditional system always be at the mercy of what we have come to call progress? Why must the southern hero who lives in the public mode always submit to the ruthlessness of the private intelligence? Or to reduce the matter to more manageable proportions, what were the flaws within the southern systems of myth and community that made the South vulnerable to the continuing encroachments of the modern age? The second question is simpler, but no less difficult. What are the technical and thematic circumstances that require *The Fathers* to shift from the pastoral quietness of its beginning to contortions of gothic horror at its end?

In answer to the larger question Tate has, of course, given us generous hints. We recall his admonition that the enslaved black man did not form a proper sort of peasantry without which there could be no great civilization. He tells us that the South had the wrong religion: a Protestantism suited to a mercantile and technological culture, when Catholicism would have better served her agrarian style. I have put these ideas simplistically and deprived them of their context, but what Tate means, as he tells us, is that the South would have been better off had it been formed along medieval lines. This is a philosophical argument and not a suggestion of what might have been in a historical sense. No one knew better than Allen Tate that the South, along with the rest of the New World, owed its very existence to the passing of the Middle Ages and to the spirit that inspired the Renaissance. Instead, what Tate says in various essays and shows us in his novel is that, seen in the context of Western history, the mythology around which southern civilization was organized was wrong.

The myth of the South as it is limned in *The Fathers* begins with the funeral of Mrs. Buchan, which occurs at the start of the book. She lies in her casket, and a sense of death pervades the house: the silence and grim stability that her condition postulates serve as background for the disorderly conduct of George Posey and the first fumbling efforts of Lacy to declare his love for young Jane. This scene is given depth and continuity by Tate's brilliant use of detail: the shoe and the petticoat that suggest a more mature sensuality and that once belonged to Lacy's mother. But most of all, there is a sense of life going on and of the maintenance of manners in the face of adversity. Major Buchan, who is torn with grief, moves through the day of the obsequies asking after and attempting to ensure the comfort of others. This is what his code demands. He must turn the face of hospitality to the world; his mourning must not be allowed to intrude upon the community. That such a system is built upon charity no one can deny, and the final proof is in the major's gentle concern for his dead wife's maid as they follow the casket up the hill to the cemetery. The funeral service itself yields its force and its sense of immediacy to the wandering thoughts of Lacy. We hear snatches of prayers, a passage from Saint Paul, a reference to the day of resurrection. Yet the reality not only of the entire sequence but of the specific scene is mundane: old Uncle Armistead uttering amens and Lacy tracing verses on the weathered stones restrain us from any flights of spirituality. The emphasis during the burial scene, like the emphasis pervading all the Buchan experience, is almost totally on the past, on ancestors long since gone to their rewards, on Lacy's sister who died before he was born. Here in the cemetery we stand literally among the fathers.

However, as Tate has often reminded us, the past is not enough. This is not to say that it is dispensable; it is not. People without history are people bereft both individually and in their institutions. As Mizener points out, whatever one thinks of the Old South, it *was* a civilization. It is possible that future generations, fully conscious of its faults, will

nonetheless celebrate it as a last pocket of organized re-
sistance against the barbarism that accompanied the passing
of the modern age. However that may be, the movement of
history engenders a series of altered circumstances. Certain
things stay essentially the same—"old verities," William
Faulkner called them—but they manifest themselves in different ways; this is one of the motives for writing at all and
one of the reasons that poets and novelists can bring fresh
visions to the same themes generation after generation. As a
study of the best literature will show, proper mythology,
based on first principles, is a device for dealing with the accidents and vicissitudes of continuing existence while holding
firmly to those truths that are unalterable.

I believe that the best and most accurate myths are religious. They take man as he is and stipulate, without flinch-
ing, human fault and all the agonies of the human condition.
Then the mythical postulation is made in terms of a metaphysical system. For example, we begin with the Eden into
which man was born, move through his fall to his redemption
by Christ, and look forward to the resurrection. Such a mythology makes bearable what Mircea Eliade calls the "terrors
of history." Man can fit himself into the terms of the myth
and see his own time and even his own individual existence
as repetitions of the larger pattern. In historical terms his
suffering is a result of the sins of his fallen fathers, but if he is
faithful he ultimately will be returned to a condition tran-
scendently better than that from which his forebears fell. In
his own life he sees the fall of man repeated in microcosm: he
is himself a sinner, and his sin must be individually redeemed
through the same sacramental system that is the salvation of
the world. The ramifications of such a mythology and its
effect on a culture that embraces it are vast, and I shall not
pursue them. But it is important to note that the fundamental delineations of the myth are not subject to modification
by the vagaries of mundane history. Man may lose his faith to
be sure, but as long as the myth prevails within a culture, it is

a source of order: usages may change, but the truths from which the usages evolve remain constant. As we learn from *The Fathers*, this did not happen in the South.

Almost from its beginnings and increasingly as the Civil War approached, the myth of the South was of a past without a future. Every aspect of life at Pleasant Hill is predicated on the customs of the fathers. The ownership of slaves, the methods of farming, the manners and forms of behavior all are inherited, and whatever relationship they once had to a complete mythical system has been largely forgotten. Things are done *now* as they were done *then* and for no other reason. Two extravagant images in the novel demonstrate the folly of clinging to a tradition based largely on the fact of its own existence, which is to say on the uses of the temporal world. I think first of that marvelous tournament sequence early in the book, which is so fully realized in the best fictional sense that the reader is swept up into it. Clearly, if one regards the matter objectively, the sight of grown men prancing around in costume and riding at rings as if they were medieval warriors is absurd. The scene is saved from being comic by Tate's skillful use of point of view: we see the action from under the pavilion, where Lacy waits with Wink Broadacre and a misused mulatto girl. But until Posey disrupts the afternoon by refusing to fight a duel with John Langdon, adult figures proceed through this chivalric travesty as in a dream.

Or consider Mr. Jarman, who has sequestered himself in the attic of the Posey house in Georgetown, his windows tightly shuttered against the diurnal march of time. He is a totally symbolic figure: he has no stake in the action; he makes nothing happen; nothing that does happen can penetrate the composure of his rarefied mind. Even the death of his sister-in-law cannot call him from the precincts of the past where he has determined to conduct his life. He knows that the best men and women have long been dead in any event. His interest is in the books he reads, all written long ago, and in the history he is writing of man's struggle for survival at the end of the Ice Age. I realize that I oversimplify Mr. Jarman in treating him merely as an image of excessive devotion to the ways of his forebears. He is part of the disorder of the Posey household, an article of the novel's gothic furniture; but along with the tournament, he helps set in perspective the myth by which Major Buchan lives and dies.

All of this is another way of getting at what Tate calls the failure of Protestantism to supply a proper mythology for the South. Whether a Catholic hegemony would have wrought a significant difference we cannot be sure, but to bring the novel closer to its religious backgrounds, think of Major Buchan's refusal to differentiate in his prayers between the welfare of his own family and the preservation of the United States. Here again distinctions of degrees of reality are blurred, and the value of human constructs is exaggerated. Christ performed his first miracle at the marriage in Cana and thereby gave the authenticity of divine sanction to the family as institution: he endorsed it as real in a fundamental sense. Another kind of ceremony was performed in Philadelphia in 1776. Neither the original declaration of principles nor the various compacts subsequently agreed on were more than political statements motivated by worldly considerations and couched in pragmatic terms. To equate the integrity of the nation with that of the family, to comprehend them as metaphysically coterminous, is to mistake that which is manufactured for that which is quintessentially real. But such was Major Buchan's and the South's error. By embracing an incomplete theology, they damaged their perceptions of final truth.

To go at this from another angle, civilization, Lacy Buchan tells us, is a common agreement to leave the abyss alone. But this is a restatement of the gnostic heresy. No societal or governmental contrivance can keep man from his folly. Manners will not save us from ourselves. The abyss yawns not before us but within us, and southern culture was viable to the extent that it recognized this truth. It would perhaps go beyond Tate's intention to suggest that the slave girl under the pavilion is a manifestation of original sin, hidden from view but not suppressed. But the South was constantly reminded of man's imperfectibility by the problems of race and slavery that to this day resist solution. I am not thinking now of slavery per se. Institutional evil brings us too quickly into the realms of abstraction. Rather, I have in mind the individual sinfulness of people that was exacerbated by the opportunities for sin afforded by slavery and the subsequent oppression of blacks. The worst of these was miscegenation, and that is why Yellow Jim is the chief catalyst. My immediate point is that the failure of Protestantism in the South was not a failure to recognize the nature of man but an inability to deal with it. Since the abyss cannot be avoided, the only way it can be dealt with individually or corporately is by a completely developed sacramental system unavailable under a Protestant dispensation. Manners, tradition, a reverence for the past, even though they be based on an accurate assessment of man's nature, are insufficient to maintain a culture through inevitable violations of the natural law.

I find it curious, in view of themes running through Allen Tate's criticism and poetry, that more has not been made of the Poseys' Catholicism. It seems to me that without either denigrating the faith or defending George Posey's morals, we might consider Catholicism as a proper spiritual background for his pragmatism. One of the *données* of the novel is Posey's obvious recognition of the limitations of the traditional system of community by which the other characters live and die. This manifests itself to Posey's discredit in his refusal to attend his mother-in-law's funeral, but he is seen in a better light as the book advances. He will not kill Langdon simply to fulfill a social requirement. He is not fooled into believing that southern gallantry will prevail over Yankee logistics. And he does not feel himself obliged by the southern code to kill Yellow Jim. None of this implies that Posey acts from any sense of piety. He does not. But I do suggest that his Catholic background saves him from some of the misapprehensions and accompanying calamities that plague most of the other characters in the novel. Nor, except for the impetuosity of Semmes, would he be subject to Susan's manipulations, which are engineered totally within the ambience of traditional southern response.

Susan's behavior is an intriguing aspect of *The Fathers*. She affords us a moment of high drama in the first section of the book by announcing her intention to marry Posey before she or those around her know whether the gunfire they have heard has meant the death of John Langdon. As we come to learn, this is impetuosity, not strength. Or rather her strength is so particular and limited that it cannot discriminate between Posey's departure from her mother's funeral and his later absences in behalf of the Confederate cause. Yet if we see her properly for what she is—the daughter of her father, an inheritor of southern tradition in all its complexity—we can comprehend the depth of her response to the disorders afflicting the house in Georgetown. The rude servants, the bad food, the improperly cleaned rooms, the carelessness of the adult Poseys for the opinions or customs of society all affront the values by which Susan has been taught to live. Caught in her own tradition, she is helpless against the violations her sense of propriety must endure in Georgetown in the same way that her father is helpless against Posey when the two face each other at Pleasant Hill. But unlike her father she cannot contain the pain of her loss within herself.

Major Buchan disowns his sons who join the Confederate army, then later kills himself to win his limited victory over the Yankee officer to whom, in his polite way, he has expressed his contempt. Thus he fulfills in his death the code by which he has lived. Susan's situation is different. She has lived her married life beyond her own people and outside her inherited tradition. In order to save her brother from marriage into the Posey family, she will go to any length, commit any crime, destroy any other human being. Her motivation, of course, is mixed. She has developed against her husband a deep and smoldering anger. She cannot or will not forgive him for having brought her to Georgetown, and the terrible climax of the novel can be read as the collapse of southern traditional behavior under the complicated moral demands of modern life. Thus she places herself in the mainstream of southern fiction. She is the spiritual relative of John Sartoris, who cannot stop killing people, and of those dark and bloody-handed characters populating the narratives of a younger generation of novelists such as William Styron, Cormac McCarthy, and Madison Jones.

Once the barrier of manners that shields us from the abyss is rent, the terror of moral darkness is compounded. In *The Fathers* only Posey can look upon and aspire to cope with the face of evil. He can do this because of the life he has lived and the theology he has been taught—whatever his beliefs may be now—by the old pinochle-playing priest or one like him. Yet I would not leave the impression that I think more highly of Posey than I do. Semmes kills Yellow Jim out of respect for and under the terms of the tradition that has guided his life. Posey murders Semmes in a flash of anger, following as always his private impulse. Both acts are wrong, but Posey's is worse: he kills for self-indulgence. Indeed, wherever blame is to be found, Posey must share it. His sale of Yellow Jim, his deception of and rudeness to the Buchan family, his abandonment of Susan to the disorders of the house in Georgetown, his acquiescence in sending young Jane to a convent, and his murder of Langdon are all evidence of his culpability and the essential destructiveness of the role he has chosen for himself. He is a prophetic and frightening figure, for the private mode is the mode of the modern world. Under its rubrics we defect from our duties as citizens, turn away from the suffering of others, and exert ourselves only in behalf of our private ends. Posey's tradition is superior to that of the Buchans, but he follows it only in the most desultory and fragmentary fashion. In abandoning his own fathers, he dooms himself.

Fragmentation, along with isolation, the spiritual and moral isolation of the individual, is another mark of our time, another theme of the literature we write and read. My final gloss on Tate's brilliant novel is to say that like all works of art its total effect is greater than its accumulated imagery. The deeply flawed tradition of the Buchans comes into contact with a vision of reality at once more real and more destructive than the southern code because it is a severely damaged version of a higher good. The result is a violence that cleanses nothing. Out of all the suffering and death comes only the promise of a bleak future summed up in Lacy Buchan's final words. "It won't make any difference if I am killed. If I am killed it will be because I love him more than I love any man."

And so have we loved him, and so have we followed him into the agonies of our present state.

The Last Agrarian: Peter Taylor
Early and Late

Few writers have staked out for themselves more narrowly defined domains than Peter Taylor. His place is middle and west Tennessee, and when a story or play is set in St. Louis or Detroit, the foreign ambience enhances the sense of southern custom. Taylor's southerners in exile remain what they are: second- and third-generation Tennessee agrarians who have made an urban progress in the world. His time is the decade of the thirties, and he is such a master of anachronism that whatever the stated date of a story may be, the attitudes and actions and details recreate the uneasy last decade of the hegemony of the southern gentry. His people are the well connected and well-to-do; the middle-class and poor and black characters who appear in his work are defined by their relationships to the wealthy. Think of the unfortunate Miss Bluemeyer in "The Death of a Kinsman," or of Jesse in "A Friend and Protector," or of the girls of the Memphis "demi-monde" in "The Old Forest."

Social distinctions are nowhere made more important than in Taylor's play *A Stand in the Mountains*. The Weavers, rich and prominent, come from Louisville to Owl Mountain for the summers; the Campbells, poor and graceless, live in the coves and eke out a living working for people such as the Weavers. But nothing can be so neat. Louisa Weaver and Thelma Campbell are matriarchs of the two parties, but their relationship has been complicated by the marriage of Louisa's son Harry to Thelma's granddaughter Lucille. This union, entered into by Harry to protest his mother's inveterate snobbishness, has incurred for both parties more misery than it has cured. Harry's brother Zack rebels against his mother's values by claiming poetry as his vocation, moving to Italy, and becoming the lover of a woman whom Louisa once tried to present to Louisville society. The action here is grim and only partially redeemed, and in his preface Taylor tells us why.

> All of the heroes and heroines in my play suffer in some degree from the emptiness of the old roles they are playing, and their suffering is increased whenever they try to make some sense out of their roles. No doubt all human beings are punished for accepting preconceived notions of their identity and of their relationship to other human beings. . . . And yet, how can anyone escape these preconceptions? In fact, the person who will always be punished most severely is he who . . . at once rejects these preconceptions and tries to continue to live amongst those who are suffering daily for their acceptance of that which he is rejecting.

Better then to escape as Zack did; but like Georgia, his mistress, who earlier has run from Louisa, he cannot stay away. They return to Owl Mountain apparently to flaunt their independence, but they become embroiled once more in all from which they thought they had freed themselves. Even to do nothing is to come off second best. Will Weaver, Louisa's brother-in-law, has refused throughout her long widowhood to pursue his love for her or even to utter it. An undistinguished historian, he has grown old writing unread books about the Indians who once lived around Owl Mountain, but his history is as empty as Zack's poetry, and his work has been his life. At the other social level things are no better. Lucille is equally as miserable in marriage as Harry, and this connecting of the two families has compromised Thelma's social position: being an in-law of the Weavers, she is no longer hired by the summer people to do domestic work.

The strains of these relationships are exacerbated by Louisa's having moved from one social role to another. The daughter of a west Tennessee preacher, she was translated to Louisville and riches as the second wife of a much older man. Since his death she has relived her life through surrogates, cousins fetched out of the country to be given debuts and conducted toward acceptable marriages. Georgia fled Louisville before the process was completed. She and Zack and Harry urge Mina, another of Louisa's Tennessee cousins, to leave before her time begins, but Mina remains loyal to Louisa.

In most of Peter Taylor's work the characters, their attitudes, and their social intercourse with one another constitute, to a great extent, the story. Typically, in *A Stand in the Mountains* the big action occurs offstage. Mina is in love with Harry; Zack is in love with Mina; Harry is in love with Georgia; but a chaste embrace is the most we see. Near the beginning Harry shoots his wife—he claims it was an accident—and near the end he kills Lucille and her grandmother and his two children and himself. Perhaps Taylor needs to shed this much blood to command our attention. In "The Old Forest," in what is almost an aside, the narrator tells of losing his two brothers in the Korean War, his mother and father in a fire, and two of his children in accidents. By ordinary standards any one of these events would be more dramatic and more moving than the search for the narrator's missing girlfriend and his fiancée's verbal exploration of caste and class in Memphis. But Taylor creates his characters so well and delves into their psyches so thoroughly that sometimes only bursts of violence will restore our awareness of a larger world beyond.

When *A Stand in the Mountains* ends, everything is in the grip of change. Georgia and Zack are returning to Italy, forced back into the aimless pattern of their itinerant life. They know now that they do not love each other very much and that their relationship and their artistic puttering travesty proper concepts of family and vocation—and are at best no less ridiculous than Will's feckless scholarship and Louisa's social conniving. Indeed Louisa will not return to Louisville: she and Will and Mina will remain on the mountain until the modern world catches up with them, which will not be very long.

As Taylor points out frequently in his work, his aristocrats are the last agrarians. They left their ruined plantations after the Civil War to engage in business or a profession in the city. They brought with them the old manners and customs, the country sense of family, or "connection," as they would put it; as we are told in "The Old Forest," what they brought from the old order "made them both better and worse than business men elsewhere." Their wives and daughters shared their values and were also better and worse and happier and unhappier than their contemporaries who broke with the past. Taylor's people know who they are; they know how they are supposed to behave; and so at the outset of their lives they have answers to the two questions that most vex the rest of the modern world. They need not search for their identities or enter into endless engagements over what is right or wrong in a given situation. But the past, any mundane past, is imperfect, and freedom is not to be found in its service. Bound by what they believe in, Taylor's characters take their stands and await their defeats.

At the end of the Civil War, Robert E. Lee was urged to lead the remnants of his army into the Virginia mountains, where his advisers believed he might hold out for however long it took the Federals to grow weary of the fight. This is the source of the title of Taylor's play. It is evident that Lee made the sensible choice in laying down his arms, but it is less certain how the last survivors of his tradition should bear themselves at the end of their losing battles. The incursion of the interstate into the country where the Indians once roamed will violate all that Will has lived for. But he has no choice in the matter, and he might as well wait on the sacred ground for this disaster to happen. After the blood that Harry has spilled,

Louisa never again can guide debutantes through a Louisville season. So she must stay with Will, and Mina will stay with her. This is right. Given the failures and dislocations of contemporary life, where would they go, what end would they seek that would be better than the conclusion they are now heirs to? We can consider this question as, at the end of the play, dialogue stops and the lights fade, leaving the stage in symbolic silence and darkness.

Taylor's plays gloss his stories in that they are more straightforward and less complicated than his fiction. Take for example "A Long Fourth" (1948), which also appears in *The Old Forest*. Harriet Wilson, matriarch and protagonist, is one of the most fatuous figures in literature. She is a caricature of everything that is or ever has been wrong with the South: a snob whose head would be empty without the prejudices that reside there. Her patronizing affection for her black cook is no more than skin-deep, and while the world engages or prepares to engage in war, her thoughts are confined to domestic niceties in general and specifically to Son's visit and the party she will give for him and Ann.

Yet, in the ambience that Taylor provides for her, Harriet is no worse than anybody else. Sweetheart, her husband, is willing to drift with history, a devoted adherent to the status quo. The daughters Helena and Kate comprehend the moral poverty of the way of life to which they were born; they complain about the narrowness of their mother's vision but, as ineffectual as their father, they protest the vicissitudes of life by smoking and occasionally drinking too much. Son and Ann are liberated from the past, but their lives are rooted in clichés different from but no more valid than those guiding Harriet. And Son, who claims at least tacitly to have outgrown the unjust attitudes of his childhood, toys with Ann's affection and exposes her to humiliation, which his sisters are glad to furnish out of boredom or malice or both.

Consider the roles the characters fill in terms of Taylor's statement of intentions in his preface to *A Stand in the*

Mountains. Harriet is wrong and does suffer because she tries to fulfill herself in the position to which she was born. But Son, who has broken the old fetters, is worse. Between him and his parents the sisters sulk, alienated from their own tradition but ignorant of any other direction their lives might follow. Ann is a southerner too, and because she has broken almost completely with her heritage, she is the most un-happy character in the story. What she has tried to suppress in her life of the mind is the one quality that Harriet has in abundance, however misdirected: a capacity for love. Conse-quently, though by this I do not imply simple cause and effect, Ann's rejection of her role has been part of her undoing.

What I have said so far makes Taylor's work appear to be formulaic, which is neither my intention nor the case. "A Long Fourth" achieves its force not only from the relation-ships of its individual characters but from the relationships of different groups of people. The initial conflict of the story is joined when Mattie, the black cook, claims the right to com-pare her affection for her nephew B. T. with Harriet's attach-ment to Son and to make them equal in their common des-tiny of having been drafted. Harriet's reprimand of Mattie over this point embarrasses the reader: clearly Harriet is not only insensitive but wrong. Yet the case is not as simple as Ann would make it when she suggests that Sweetheart help B. T. buy a farm. There is no evidence that B. T. wants a farm; he appears to be happy living in his cabin behind the Wilsons' house, getting drunk on Saturday night and bringing home dissolute women. Those most in need of reforming some-times do not want to be reformed, and not everyone has ambi-tion. In this story blacks and whites are locked together not so much in mutual dependence but—as we have seen in a thousand other southern stories and novels—in mutual doom.

The whole story is seen in the context of a war that left the world in spiritual and cultural disorder from which it has yet to recover. The point is not to assert that the old order was

particularly good, but to ask whether what replaced it is nec-
essarily better. To take such a cautionary view of life is salu-
tary because it is accurate. I do not want to suggest that Peter
Taylor's stories are reactionary or gloomy: they are neither.
But fiction seeks to tell the truth; one truth is that we move
from one set of morally skewed and unjust conventions to
another, and another is that we learn more from and comprehend ourselves more fully in images of the past than of the
present—which repeats a truism that applies to all of the best
southern writing. Taylor is the youngest and chronologically
the last of the writers of the Southern Renascence, born late
but in time to see the Old South's twilight, the crepuscular
moment when the old social values stood balanced against
the new, though on a scale reduced from that of Warren or
Faulkner. Still his vision is complete and achieves, I think, its
fullest fruition in *A Woman of Means* (1950).

In this novella, as in most of Taylor's other work, the past
defines the present; but Gerald Dudley, a widower with a
twelve-year-old son, does not typify Taylor's business and
professional men. When the narrative begins he is a salesman, afire with ambition; and except for a few sentimental
memories that he is willing to keep, he is eager to shed his
country ways and forget his country background. He is hu-
miliated when his date reprimands him for wearing brown
shoes with his tuxedo, and although he permits Quint to
spend summers on a Tennessee farm with his grandmother,
he lays down rules governing what Quint should be allowed
to do and see. He will not hear Mrs. Lovell's argument that it
is good for children to be raised in the country. Yet what but
an affection for his own rural past would prompt him to tell
Quint to take off his shoes and walk in the wet grass "so you
can remember what it feels like"?

Gerald becomes an executive in the hardware company for
which he works, moves to St. Louis, and marries the woman
of means; but because she is city-bred and cosmopolitan, a
divorcée schooled in the ways of the world, he is never com-

fortable with her. He loves her, to be sure, and loves her daughters by her previous marriage; but he never understands them, never really trusts them. They are women and therefore mysterious; but more than this, they have no knowledge of the social conventions that well-bred Memphis and Nashville girls would have been taught from the cradle. For all three women the sense of family, so important in the South, has been distorted. Ann has been made skittish and possessive by the failure of her first marriage. The girls are loyal to their own father as well as to their mother and stepfather; because they are independently wealthy, they are ultimately beyond their mother's control. When Laura, home from school in the East, fails to treat Gerald with the courtesy he thinks is due him, relationships begin to disintegrate.

Laura's offense is about as small as it could be, a matter of manners exquisitely defined, but Gerald's southern sensibilities are offended; and when the girls return for Christmas, he refuses to attend their parties, claiming the urgency of business. Indeed his business is in trouble, and readers who find patterns of southern behavior incomprehensible can see in Gerald's impending dismissal as president of his company sufficient motivation for his coldness to the girls. Believe what you will about the ghosts of agrarian custom, they nevertheless haunt Gerald and drive his life and finally help to rob Ann of her sanity. In his insistence that the family must live on his reduced pay, she discovers another kind of masculine betrayal.

They must, Gerald tells Ann, leave the grand house her father built for her and move into an apartment that he can afford. Quint will be withdrawn from St. Louis Country Day and enrolled in a public school. According to Gerald's code, for him and Quint to be supported by a woman is not proper. But what of Ann? For Gerald to return to the life he lived before he and Ann were married is one thing, but she has never known this life, which her past makes insupportable. She cannot go with him, but she cannot endure the thought of

losing him and Quint. She begins her plunge into incurable
mental illness, the first and enduring symptom of which is
her false claim that she is pregnant. She fantasizes that she
will have a boy to replace Quint.

Yet the situation is still more complicated. In this confrontation between tradition and modernity that drives Ann insane, no one is blameless. Early in the action Ann wonders
aloud to Quint whether Gerald might have married her for
her money. In a world where values are predominantly mate-
rialistic, such a question is bound to arise and to remain a
shadowy presence. The code under which Gerald lives was
developed in part to allay such suspicions. As cruel as
Gerald's decision not to live on Ann's money seems, it must
be balanced against Laura's concern with her own beauty,
Bess's engagement to a band leader, and the general indifference of the girls and their father—and to a certain extent
Ann—toward the forms that in Gerald's view define civilized
society.

The key to the proper reading of this story is Quint. He is
the narrator, less an actor in the main thrust of the narrative
than an innocent observer who comes to knowledge at the
end. Captivated by the warmth of his new family, who in the
beginning feel genuine affection for one another, he drifts
away from the traditions that rule his father's life without
realizing that he is doing so. Or perhaps he is induced into a
change of heart by the love and need of his stepmother. She
says that she has always wanted a son, and she feels that a son
might have saved her first marriage. Quint returns her love
and at times shares her mystification at his father's behavior.

At the end, when Ann is to go to a sanitarium in Connec-
ticut to be near the girls who are moving east and the house is
to be torn down and sold piecemeal, Quint's allegiance has
been claimed by the modern dispensation. While his father
and Bess discuss her planned marriage and blame each other
for what has happened to Ann, Quint reads over and over the
newspaper account of Charles Lindbergh's successful flight

across the Atlantic. In the future Quint will live once more in a boardinghouse with his father; perhaps he will visit his grandmother on the farm, but this will not touch him. From the start, it is now clear, Quint has belonged more than he realized to his stepmother and to her culture; but he knows by the novel's end that the agrarian age has ended, and his eyes are on a future that will be increasingly technological.

A Summons to Memphis takes Taylor farther from his home base than he usually allows himself to travel. His narrator, Philip Carver, though originally from Nashville and Memphis, now lives in New York. Philip's father, George, an octogenarian when the novel begins, is spiritually adrift because he was betrayed forty years earlier by his best friend, Lewis Shackleford. At the failure of Shackleford's firm, for which George Carver works, he moves his family from Nashville to Memphis. His wife immediately takes to her bed and withdraws from society. Carver, with little apparent motive beyond his bitterness toward Shackleford, frustrates in succession the marriage plans of his two daughters and his son, causing the daughters to remain spinsters and the son to leave the South. Now a widower, he intends to remarry, and Philip is called to Memphis to help prevent the old man's wedding as George earlier had prevented theirs.

Philip Carver is not a typical Taylor character. His translation to a job in publishing and a Manhattan flat shared with a Jewish woman from Cleveland seems to have dulled his personality. Making a reluctant passage home, he is uncertain until his plane lands whether he will help his sisters or his father. Since George is at the airport to meet him, he decides he will "stand up" with George; but the intended bride has left Memphis, having been subverted by the sisters. The next family crisis and the next summons to Memphis come when George, having made up his differences with Lewis Shackleford, wants to pay him an extended visit. This time Philip sides with his sisters, but the sudden death of Shackleford renders any loyalty or action supererogatory.

A Summons to Memphis gives the impression of being at once old and unfinished, as if it were written in the early seventies—when the main action takes place—and resurrected fifteen years later without revision. The book is loosely constructed, often repetitive, and one of the characters, Philip's brother who has died in World War II, is too little a human being, too much a symbol. An editor should have repaired these defects. Of more importance are the uncertainty of George's motives and Philip's fecklessness. Compared with Son in "A Long Fourth," another southern expatriate, Philip seems flat; but Son and Philip exist in different worlds. In 1939 the agrarian South was doomed, but it lived in the manners and affections of Sweetheart and other business and professional men of Memphis and Nashville. It was shared by their wives and children. By the seventies the last survivors of the old dispensation are either dead or too old to continue the struggle, and southern custom endures only in such private confrontations as those Taylor delineates here.

Yet the novel embodies a public dimension in an irony that Taylor has not exploited previously. The lives of all the Carvers are distorted by the failure of Lewis Shackleford's business, but it was his success, and the success of others like him, that eradicated the influence of southern agrarianism. Shackleford's character is based on Rogers Caldwell, and Taylor follows his prototype faithfully. In 1917 Caldwell founded the first investment banking firm in the South. When his financial empire collapsed in 1930 he barely escaped prison. But like Shackleford, by the end of his life Caldwell was considered a financial genius; and invitations to his Saturday luncheons were prized by Nashville businessmen. His ambition became the common ambition, as the agrarian twilight faded into darkness. What is left by the seventies are remnants—manners privately practiced, standards privately held.

In *A Summons to Memphis* the demise of southern society is seen in the flamboyant dress and suggestive conversation of the aging Carver sisters, in George's dates with young women and his visits to discotheques, in Philip's alienation from home and tradition. He and his girlfriend from Cleveland see their parents as part of the graying of America, the geriatric crisis that concerns us all. And when Philip's boyhood friend suggests that he give his collection of rare books to a Memphis university, he can only laugh. For him there is no more Memphis, no more family, no more South. Thus the story Peter Taylor has been telling all his writing life reaches its proper end.

Like any other writer Taylor has his weaknesses. Much of his work is written in the first person, and he does not always resist the temptation to self-indulgence that this point of view presents. "The Old Forest," successful though it is, is too long: the narrator is allowed to express too many opinions, to go on at too great length about the social situation out of which the story develops. He is tedious at times. In other stories—I think of "Porte Cochère" and "Promise of Rain"— characters seem directed more by moods and inherent disposition than by motivation. The social conventions that inform most of his fiction are of scant use to him in the wartime setting of "Promise of Rain," and they become too rarefied to support significant action in "Porte Cochère."

Peter Taylor's canvas is small, not because his usual form is the short story but because he lacks the range of, for instance, V. S. Pritchett, who can spin tales about undertakers or antique dealers or lords of the manor with equal authority and grace. But as Taylor has often said, a writer is as good as his best work; and the Peter Taylor of *A Woman of Means* and many of his stories is very good indeed.

Richard Weaver and the Bishop's Widow: A Cautionary Tale

In the summer of 1958, one of the students in my fiction-writing class was the widow of an Episcopal bishop, a tautology concerning which Evelyn Waugh made much merriment. She was a lady of advanced middle age, filled with energy and good intentions, and she resisted instruction as adamantly as any student I ever encountered. She was willing to try to use concrete details, to give her narratives beginnings, middles, and ends, and reluctantly to establish conflict of a mild order. But in spite of the thousands of Episcopal sermons she must have heard—I assume that the spouses of bishops attend services—she refused in the face of all cajolery, argument, or threat to entertain the idea of original sin. I quoted Robert Penn Warren to the effect that you could not write a novel about your sainted grandmother unless you could find some old letters that proved your grandfather was not who you thought he was. The bishop's widow happily replied that she was certain I had misunderstood Mr. Warren. I gave her Tolstoy's line about happy families being all alike, I cited Aristotle, but nothing worked. She continued to create characters who were free of fault and immune to error—her heroes sanctified from the start, her villains eager for conversion. As a last resort, I made an appeal to Richard Weaver.

In the spring of 1958, Dick Weaver had participated in a literary program at Vanderbilt. He had read his essay "Contemporary Southern Literature," not quite in its entirety, but in a sufficiently full version, and one day after class I invited the bishop's widow to listen to a tape of Weaver's lecture. She accepted cheerfully, agreeable as always except in the matter of innate sinfulness, and she and I spent a long hour of a summer afternoon listening to Weaver praise southern writers for their understanding of the human condition. Unlike the Transcendentalists, who thought people were by nature good, and unlike the naturalists, who saw men and women as victims of circumstances, southern writers, Weaver insisted, knew that we all are flawed at conception and stand constantly in need of ethical and spiritual redemption. Weaver said more than this, of course. He listed the causes of the Southern Renascence that have since become a part of scholarly convention: the homogeneous society; the connection with the land; the sense of a concrete history; the feudal structure of the society; the religion, practiced formally on Sunday and experienced continually in the relationship of an agrarian people to the natural world. But in his listing of southern literary virtues, Weaver put a belief in original sin first: it informed all other facets of southern understanding.

The bishop's widow was astonished. Where my renditions of Warren and Tolstoy and Aristotle had fallen on unfertile ground, Weaver's rhetoric took root. She could not deny what she had heard or twist Weaver's carefully built sentences into meanings that he did not intend. Clearly he believed what he believed, and for a while after the tape had run, the bishop's widow sat in silent bemusement. "Well," she said finally. "I *am* surprised. I thought you were the only person left in the world who thought that way."

"Oh no," I replied, with as much conviction as I could achieve, still hoping to help improve her work, but secretly I half agreed with her. Many believed in evil, but few believed in sin. Weaver and I, his fellow traveler, were a minority then as now: right or wrong, we were out of step with the rest of creation.

Richard Weaver was the Saint Paul of the Vanderbilt Agrarians. He was born too late to be one of the twelve, but with the possible exception of Donald Davidson, he became the movement's most vigorous and eloquent defender. In the early forties, when most of the surviving contributors to *I'll Take My Stand* were turning their attention to other matters, Weaver took up the cause of southern culture with a constancy that never wavered and a skill that he honed in his two best and best-known books.

In *Ideas Have Consequences* Weaver demonstrated that concepts hatched in the thin air of a seminar room or the silence of a philosopher's study make their way sooner or later into the public mind, where in some instances they engender action. Descartes was the spiritual father of the Enlightenment that issued into the French Revolution. Hegel conceived his dialectic, and Marx turned it into a blueprint for Communist terror. But, as *The Ethics of Rhetoric* shows, ideas live in the words of rhetoricians. Lincoln constructing his political career, Clarence Darrow defending the right to teach evolution in the public schools of Tennessee, Burke pleading the causes of Catholics and American colonists, all in their different ways put ideas to work in behalf of specific ends. So much of what Weaver said in these two books has come into our common understanding that it is easy to forget that he said it first. Television news advances the case of one or another ideology that has made a progress from the scholarly article to the textbooks to the reporter's script—just as Weaver said it was doing and would continue to do. Almost constantly, ideas shaped by rhetoric have consequences in the public mind and in public action. Yet Weaver remains a prophet largely without honor partly because he was a conservative who worked in a liberal ambience, but partly too because of his extraordinary loyalty to the Agrarian cause.

In 1956, when the surviving Fugitives gathered at Vanderbilt to talk over old times, only Davidson still shared with Weaver an untempered faith in the principles set forth in *I'll Take My Stand*. John Crowe Ransom, who in the thirties had defended Agrarianism in public debate, now concluded that the movement had been a mistake: he referred to it as a pursuit of a "lost cause" and said the Fugitives should have stuck to their poetry instead of engaging in social criticism and politics. On the eve of publication of the manifesto, Robert Penn Warren had objected to the title because it seemed to present the book as a belligerent defense of the Old South. And in the essay that he published in *I'll Take My Stand*, as well as in many later utterances, Allen Tate said that neither the Old South nor the postbellum South furnished a cultural paradigm because the southern religion was the wrong one for what the Agrarians had in mind. This was an important point, and Weaver's failure to engage it weakens his essays on the South and, in some cases, renders them irrelevant in spite of the logic of his arguments and the clarity of his prose.

For Weaver, the good society was the feudal society as it existed in France before the revolution. Steeped in the observations of Alexis de Tocqueville, he feared a tyranny of both majority and minority; he saw as the logical antidote a class system patterned on that of the three estates of the ancien régime, the levels of society balancing each other and operating in consort to prevent an unsalutary domination by any group. In view of what is now known about prerevolutionary France, this idea seems less naïve than it might have when Weaver wrote almost fifty years ago. Recent studies show that the Bourbon kings and the aristocracy, though guilty of many excesses, were not as oppressive as earlier historians accused them of being and that the worst of their faults pale beside the persecutions and genocide of the Terror. The French population was 90 percent Catholic before the revolution, but the largest group put to death by the revolutionaries were priests and nuns and the laity who supported them. Like present students of the French Revolution—Pierre Chaunu for example—Tate understood that the attack on religion by the Jacobins was an assault on the foundations of Western civilization.

Weaver also understood this to a degree. He judged religion to be a principal root of southern culture, but it was a religion without liturgy or sacrament. While Tate was writing to Davidson that in his view only the Catholic faith could rescue the world from barbarism, Davidson, like Weaver, agreed with him in general but clung to the idea of religion as only one aspect of southern culture, a part among other equal parts, and he and Weaver were content to describe it in terms almost as amorphous as those used to define the Transcendental system that Weaver abhorred. In "Contemporary Southern Literature," Weaver wrote that the South "is a world of place and time, but it is also a world which includes the mystery of the timeless. It is a place in which the transcendental is apprehended in the actual, and the actual is never without some link to the transcendental. The real and the ideal, the act and the idea, man as he is and man as he ought to be, nature and supernature are presented in their inextricable involvement." And later in the same essay he notes, "As I cross the Ohio River on my way to the South, I have a feeling that I am entering a region where things are somehow known mysteriously."

Like almost everything else Weaver said about the pre–World War II South, this was true. Agrarian life fostered a belief in the supernatural, and the South was a rural community—for a while. But with the Second World War began the exodus to the city. The first wave went to work in defense plants, and some of them remained because they liked their new environment. Others, who would have preferred to continue farming, found on their return from service that the farm could no longer support them. Cotton pickers and combines, herbicides and increasingly powerful tractors allowed one tiller of the earth to do the work of ten. The nine who were displaced had no option except to seek employment in the cities. When this happened, the source or religion in the lives of these people was left behind; a mystery that resided in the agrarian world was not transportable.

But all this is hindsight, a criticism of Weaver not for what he saw but for his failure to foresee some of the specifics of a dark future that he foresaw well in general terms. His description of the South before World War II is as good as any we have and more accurate than most. He was among the first to understand the Southern Renascence for what it was, a literary movement born out of the common elements of a culture—the homogeneity of the people, the love of the land, and of course the sense of mystery. Whatever differences in attitude and background the southern writers of the first half of this century brought to their work, they all were heirs to these elements of the southern heritage, which became the bases of their work. Warren, Kentucky smalltown boy and Rhodes scholar, and Faulkner, veteran of the Royal Canadian Air Force who learned to fly after the war was over, were in most aspects of their upbringing and personalities quite different. But they shared the southern legacy that Weaver described and understood, and this was the source of their literary strength. The achievements of Stark Young and Thomas Wolfe and Roark Bradford, of Allen Tate and William Alexander Percy and John Gould Fletcher are equally a product of their southernness. The common history of all these writers bound them together and enhanced their literary gifts.

In 1957 Donald Davidson pointed out that though the history and temper of the South were indeed as Weaver had described them, the Southern Renascence began only after the southern tradition had begun to decay. Great literary movements came, Davidson said, at times of cultural transition, when the old dispensation lived in a state of tension beside whatever new system would replace it. He cited Periclean Greece, Renaissance England, and the modern South. The tradition had to be threatened to bring forth its artistic fruit, which meant that it had to die, though Davidson did not go so far as to say this. Weaver, living in exile in Chicago, gave scant attention to the decline of southern culture. He could, as he said, feel the difference between North and South when he crossed the Mason-Dixon Line. What he found when in the summers he returned to Weaverville, North Carolina, was so different from what he observed on the University of Chicago campus, where he spent the academic year, that the contrast between the two places perhaps blinded him to changes taking place in his native land. At his death in 1963 he was still proclaiming that the South as he knew and loved it would endure.

"The Southern Tradition," published posthumously in 1964, is one of Weaver's best essays. In it he began with a declaration that the proper role of the South was to be what he then conceived it to be: "the Solid South," separate in spirit and mind from the rest of the nation with much wisdom to offer all who were willing to listen. To support this assertion, he undertook to explain the South in terms of its history. Unlike other sections of the United States, it never "seceded from European culture." Southern unity was molded by the Civil War, and southerners continued to believe that their part in that struggle was honorable, because history and the Constitution were on their side. They lost because they were outnumbered, not outfought, and their sufferings in battle and during Reconstruction brought them close to each other.

Then, years after Ransom had in his decorous way repudiated his role in the Agrarian movement, Weaver resurrected Ransom's image of the Georgia farmer, sitting on the fence rail and chewing on a straw, as the moral superior to a salesman in Detroit. However far from the fold Ransom may have strayed, Weaver remained a true believer, and he devoted much of the last half of "The Southern Tradition" to a defense of *I'll Take My Stand* and of the South therein described that he believed would endure. Outsiders, Weaver said, might expect the South with the passage of time to conform in custom and spirit to the rest of the nation. But Weaver thought otherwise: "The South is one of those entities to which one can apply the French saying, 'the more it changes the more it remains the same.'"

Weaver's considerable contribution to the intellectual history of our century grew out of his ability to see things as they were, to describe the world he lived in accurately, and to predict where the excesses that he claimed were part of northern culture would lead. Several years ago, but too late for Weaver to have read it, Russell Kirk said that our universities had turned into insane asylums, of which the administrators and professors were not the keepers but the chief inmates. More recently others—William Bennett, Irving Kristol, Allan Bloom—have confirmed this appraisal, and anyone who is interested in the matter can gather evidence for himself. Our classes in ethics teach that there are no ethics; our classes in literature teach that there is no literature; even our scientists allow ideology to intrude upon their thought.

If Weaver had lived, he surely would have updated his work on the development of ideas to show how those Cartesian and Kantean and Hegelian principles that he distrusted from the beginning had incubated in the work of Nietzsche and Wittgenstein and Heidegger and come to fruition—though this is a strikingly inapt word to apply to the situation—in the mutterings of Merleau-Ponty and Derrida. And he would have been distressed to discover that the South had not been spared. He would have observed for example the transformation of southern politics as manifested in the Johnson and Carter administrations, and he would have had to make a reassessment, not of his values, but of the South. And indeed, we need his vision and his skill to sort out our present situation. The end of the South as a distinctly different part of the United States has been declared annually by people of various literary and political persuasions; I have been among them.

But the South hangs on in recognizable form. The good old boys are still with us; we still have our manners and our sense of humor; we remain the Bible Belt. But we are becoming citified. Country music seems to live as much in the hearts of truck drivers as in those of farmers; our land is being cleared to make way for factories. Something has been lost, and the deprivation can be seen in our literature. Are Barry Hannah and Harry Crews and Cormac McCarthy *really* southern novelists? If so, is the South *really* still the South?

I no longer believe, as I once did, that I can answer these questions, and Weaver is no longer with us to point the way. But he has a disciple in Marion Montgomery, who attempts to resolve the dilemma by redefining what a southerner is. Montgomery is learned and articulate; indeed, he is bursting at the seams with knowledge, all of which he wants to share with you. He sounds as if he had been locked in a library for the last twenty years with no one to talk to and no materials with which to write. In his expanded version of his 1986 Lamar lectures—to have delivered them as they are printed would have required about three hours each—he follows every turning in every road to the point that the main thrust of his argument is sometimes overwhelmed by his divagations. But mainly he clings to the definition of the South as a geographical location, while bestowing southern citizenship on those who believe in his spiritual principles and excluding those who do not believe, wherever they were born.

Among Montgomery's honorary southerners are Saint Augustine and Saint Thomas Aquinas, Jacques Maritain, Étienne Gilson, Eric Voegelin, and T. S. Eliot. The list could be expanded, but not so far that it would include a single name whose work I do not admire. Montgomery's heroes are my heroes. His views of what is wrong and right in our civilization are largely my views. And I share his admiration for southerners who are such by birth as well as by conviction: Weaver and Davidson, Allen Tate and Flannery O'Connor. Montgomery also expresses admiration for Ransom and Warren, but his is a selective approval that does not engage the late work of either. According to Augustinian principles, we who love the same things should live in charity with and admiration for each other. I do admire Marion Montgomery, but I confess to being befuddled by a system that attempts to answer Tate's objection to the southern religion by claiming that Thomists are Confederates at heart.

Still, there is some historical justification for Montgomery's view. It is not widely known—and at this late date few Catholics probably want it known—that in 1860 the Catholic hierarchy, north and south, were almost solidly against abolition. There were two reasons for this: though they did not believe in slavery and said so repeatedly, they conceived the abrupt end of the system as an invitation to chaos; and they had no reason to trust the abolitionists, having suffered at their hands almost as much vilification and calumny as the South had had to endure. Father Abraham Ryan became the unofficial poet laureate of the Confederacy and served, like many of his fellow priests, as an unofficial chaplain to the army, the Confederate government having made no provision for chaplains despite the fact that one of their generals was an Episcopal bishop.

But as I have accused Montgomery of doing, I take us astray. Allen Tate and Flannery O'Connor combined the Catholic and southern traditions. But Eliot and Maritain did not combine them, nor did Ransom or Faulkner or Warren. The weakness inherent in trying to force the two traditions upon each other is demonstrated by Montgomery's failure to take up the case of Walker Percy, who is southern by birth and Catholic by conversion. Percy's work is distinctly southern in that he uses southern landscapes and characters who follow the mores and speak the language of the South. But unlike Faulkner and Eudora Welty and to some extent O'Connor, he does not develop his themes and the truth he tells from his southern ambience. Despite the presence in his work of red-neck sheriffs and heavy-drinking gentlemen, the dimensions of reality that he probes are delineated in European philosophy and in a religious system alien to most of the South.

Percy should be the perfect exemplar of a southern-born southerner, a "prophetic poet," as Montgomery likes to call writers who recognize absolutes and deal with eternal themes. But as in Tate's late work, the southern element in Percy's writing seems almost epiphenomenal to his Christian concerns. Most of his fiction is set in Louisiana, and it is fun for it to take place there because of southern habits and idiosyncrasies in themselves interesting. If the action of his novels were in Minnesota or Oregon, the work would doubtless suffer, but the stories could still be told and the themes could still be pursued, which is not the case with *Absalom, Absalom!* or *The Ponder Heart*. The amalgamation of southern and Catholic traditions results in a diminution of the southern element and calls for a new definition of the South.

I do not find this definition in Montgomery's book, but it is useful and rich and, as he would like to think, "prophetic" in many ways. He is certainly right to invoke the ghosts of Donald Davidson and Richard Weaver when he examines the deficiencies of modern society and gropes for paths to lead us back to spiritual roots. Davidson was among the most loyal defenders of everything that was traditionally southern; he was Procrustean; he never gave an inch. Near the end of his life, years after his daughter and son-in-law had become Catholic converts, he told Allen Tate that he had come to see that Catholicism had to be supported, though he chose to lend his support while remaining outside the fold. Weaver's situation is more difficult to assess, since he died believing that the South would hold out against the material and spiritual temptations of the modern world.

With Davidson's eager collaboration, Randall Stewart, then head of the Vanderbilt English department, invited Weaver to be a visiting professor there in 1964–1965. Weaver accepted readily. We at Vanderbilt hoped that this would be the first step in making Weaver a permanent member of our faculty, which of course he understood. He looked forward to coming to Nashville. The last letter I received from him was largely concerned with where he would live. He wanted, if it were available, a suite in an apartment hotel with a coffee shop where he could get breakfast. There was such a place hardly a block from the campus, but Dick was never to occupy it. He died in the spring of 1963, and there is no way to know how the friendly environment of Vanderbilt might have affected his work or what new vision of the South he might have had as he watched the unfolding of history. We can be sure only that whatever he said would have been logical and cogently rendered.

But he would not have convinced everybody. The bishop's widow went to her grave a devoted disciple of Rousseau.

Southern Writers in Spiritual Exile

In 1935 forty writers and critics, most of whom would earn some measure of literary fame, gathered in Baton Rouge to discuss southern letters. In reading over the record of that meeting—or that part of the record published in the spring, 1985, issue of the *Southern Review*—I was struck by the fact that the participants had little if anything to say about why the South was in the midst of a literary renascence. Hard things were said about university administrators and even harder things about publishers, most of which might justly be repeated today. But there was scant discussion of literary theory because, after all, those participants were producing the work, writing the poetry and fiction that was the stuff of the renascence, and movements can hardly be dissected and subjected to theory until they are over or until a significant phase of the movement is complete.

Whether or not the renascence ended after the Second World War, the theorizing about it began then. The most commonly accepted theory of why the South had produced and to some degree was still producing great literature was basically agrarian. The argument, articulated best by Richard Weaver and Donald Davidson, went like this: Life lived on the farm is more authentic than life lived in the city, because the rural experience teaches the nature of reality. In the city one is insulated from the elements; those who work the land learn from the weather and from experience with the land. Although, according to the agrarian theory, farmers are the most contented of people, conditions never suit them. It either doesn't rain or rains too much. The spring is too cold or comes too soon. Mules are contrary, and tractors break down. This is only the beginning of a litany of troubles that any experienced farmer has on the tip of his tongue. But these very vicissitudes contribute to bucolic fulfillment. The agrarian sees how things work. He knows nature and therefore knows reality firsthand in a way that the city dweller can never know it.

What I like most about this theory leads me to a question that I have been pondering and attempting to write about for many years. In 1970 I published in the *Southern Review* an essay entitled "Death by Melancholy," in which I attempted to trace the loss of a sense of the transcendent in modern society and the effect that this loss had on literature, particularly that of the South. I began then as now with agrarianism, because it has always seemed to me that the most telling argument offered in behalf of rural life is that it develops a sense of piety. Southern religion was thought to be connected with, perhaps an outgrowth of, the southern experience of planting and harvesting. It was, Allen Tate maintained, the wrong religion, Protestant when it should have been Catholic, but it still served southern writers very well. It was so much a part of the culture that it was taken for granted. Most of the poems produced during the high renascence were secular in theme, as were almost all the novels. Frequently no character in a piece of fiction ever entered a church or claimed a religious affiliation or referred to God except to swear. But there were enough church scenes and enough prayers said in the novels and sufficient references to Scripture in the poetry to demonstrate that the renascence was rooted in a Christian ambience.

Now what happens when the Christian ambience ceases to exist? My argument in "Death by Melancholy" was that society develops an impulse toward self-destruction, a death wish that manifests itself paradoxically in a frenzied worship of life. In the late sixties, when I was developing this theory, we had freed ourselves from old behavioral restraints that were religious in origin and had replaced our lost belief with a new freedom, as we termed it, to make love with anyone at any time in any way under any circumstances. This had many ramifications of course. The unrestrained pursuit of physical satisfactions leads to the abuse of almost everything but, most important, free love imperils the family as an organizing institution of society and as a central force in maintaining and conveying a sense of the sacred. Also, since the young and the beautiful are considered the best lovers, our understanding of the rhythms of human existence was distorted by the advent of a cult of perpetual youth as evidenced by the building of thousands of health clubs; the enrichment of the man who invented the Nautilus exercise machine, who incidentally has had many wives, each younger than the one previous; the publication of innumerable diet books; the sale of hundreds of millions of jogging costumes; and the full employment of legions of plastic surgeons. In such a society no pleasures are reserved for old age. Since there is no way to win at time's game, we became as we aged a people of sorrows; our lives were bereft of meaning, and our very efforts to stay young forever were symptoms of a moral sickness that propelled us toward death. So went my argument in 1970.

But times change. With the end of the Vietnam War and the reassessment of the implications of our involvement that followed, there has been in our society a moral as well as a political disengagement. A few protesters are still left, a few voices are still raised in behalf of this or that cause, but most people, young and old alike, are tending to their own affairs. Religious and political leaders who urge us to work for social reforms are left with diminished followings. I suspect that one reason for our moral indifference is our loss of a belief in absolutes. Bereft of commonly held first principles, almost any intelligent and articulate person can take either side of almost any issue and compose an argument as convincing and logical as that of his counterpart on the other side, but not more so. This state of ethical confusion issues into the moral detachment of which I speak, and this has great consequences for literature and for those who write it.

Literature ought to mean something; novels and stories and poems ought to be informed with a view of reality, with some kind of belief in, or at least attitude toward, the human condition and the truths that underlie it. I am not thinking of programmatic literature, of works that set out to prove a preconceived theme. Writing is a process of discovery, a way for the author to determine in essence who he is and what he thinks: writers start with questions, not answers. A writer of fiction will begin with a concept of a character about whom he wants to know more or with a situation that he wants to pursue, with what James called the "germ" of the story. But to find out who he is and what he thinks, the writer has to be somebody and to think something to begin with. I am speaking not merely of time and place, of social ambience or historical position, but of ethical orientation and a sense of the sacred. In literature, as elsewhere, nothing comes of nothing. An emptiness in the heart and soul of the artist leads to an emptiness at the center of the art itself. The creative process can discover and develop and define only what already exists in rudimentary form within the being of the artist.

For example, Flannery O'Connor and Bobbie Ann Mason have similar styles and write about similar situations. O'Connor's involvement with the grotesque was greater than Mason's, but Mason has the same ear for dialogue and the same eye for detail that O'Connor had, and she is interested in the same kind of people. Her talent and technical virtuosity equal O'Connor's. The difference between them is one of moral commitment and religious belief. O'Connor's work is too familiar to require exegesis. We need think only of the religious imagery that permeates her stories and novels, of the Christian rituals that appear in them, and of the Christian doctrine that is at the heart of every significant scene. There are pictures of Christ and images of the Holy Spirit and peacocks and lambs and visions of ghostly processions into heaven. There are baptisms and last rites, sermons and symbolic fires; these set the tone for a religious vision that informs all the events and characters in the O'Connor canon. Take away the Christian intention from O'Connor's fiction and you have left a human menagerie, a collection of hollow-headed and willful people who are largely unsympathetic. Or we are left with a body of literature that except for its heavier emphasis on violence is similar to the fiction of Bobbie Ann Mason.

In Mason's "Shiloh," there are Leroy and Norma Jean and Norma Jean's mother, Mabel. Leroy is a truck driver incapacitated by a wreck, Norma Jean sells cosmetics at the Rexall drugstore, Mabel works in an upholstery shop and spends her free time visiting her daughter, giving free advice and snooping around the premises. The story is about the death of love, the disintegration of a marriage nourished at first by Leroy's long absences as he drove his truck around the country. Forced to be with her husband for an extended period, Norma Jean falls out of love. What we have here is a kind of no-fault fiction. People come together, pair off, get married, then get divorced, but no serious commitment is made at the wedding and nothing of enduring value is lost when the marriage fails. Deprived of its sacramental quality, literature ceases to be art and becomes artifice. In a morally detached world, neither Leroy and Norma Jean nor their marriage has any significance beyond the clever surface details and the ingenious dialogue that Mason is able to conjure up. Norma Jean lifts weights, studies English composition, plays an electric organ; Leroy builds model houses with Popsicle sticks, watches television, smokes pot. The text is peppered with brand names of products, titles of songs and movies and TV programs—the nomenclature of the lower middle class.

Mabel calls a dachshund a "datsun," and tells how one

chewed off a baby's leg. Both of his wife and strangers, Leroy asks, "What do you think?" but the question is rhetorical: he seeks no opinion, has no specific topic in mind. Norma Jean, chagrined to have been caught smoking by her mother, says: "She don't know the meaning of the word knock. . . . It's a wonder she hadn't caught me years ago." Mabel urges Norma Jean and Leroy to visit the battlefield at Shiloh. She suggests that Norma Jean might join the United Daughters of the Confederacy. But the past means nothing to any of Mason's characters. Shiloh, Mabel thinks, is a place to repair her daughter's dying marriage, but at Shiloh, where the cemetery reminds Leroy of a subdivision site, the marriage and the story come to an end. Whatever meaning is here is on the surface. Unlike the fiction of O'Connor, in which underlying meanings are significant and the vision is apocalyptic, in Mason's work everything is on the surface: what you see is what you get.

When the commonly held sense of the sacred is lost, you can shout as Flannery O'Connor did, but you have to have something to shout about; therein lies the difficulty. If you are devout, as O'Connor was, you can work from your own sense of the divine, but if you do not have the sacred within yourself, your work is in jeopardy because society will no longer furnish it for you. Or at least this was what I thought when I wrote "Death by Melancholy" those many years ago. I am not prepared yet to abandon that position, but I should like to modify it. Until the recent past, the basic question that most writers asked themselves—and that admits of innumerable variations—was, "How do you feel about God?" You could be for God, against God, disgusted with God, indifferent to God; you could believe or not believe. But the act of asking the question established a connection, no matter how tenuous, between the writer and the spiritual dimension that has informed Western literature for thousands of years. A conscious decision not to believe is in a way an act of devotion: to take the time to ask the question is to recognize the importance of what is being asked about. Now, in our state of moral detachment, we are no longer asking the question. Caught up in material concerns, in hedonistic and acquisitive impulses, we have transferred our faith to secular millennialism, which is a form of gnosticism. Despite the failure throughout history of every human scheme devised to bring about the enduring happiness of mankind, we as writers and intellectuals place our trust in social programs and political action without reference to whether there is a divine element in the circumstances under which we live. But this is another subject. The point I wish to make here is that those writers who continue to ask about the existence and nature of the transcendent are better writers than those who do not.

One of the most prominent novelists to emerge in the last twenty-five years is Cormac McCarthy. Although one suspects he is a former altar boy, he was done with God before he ever put pen to paper, and he writes as if he has taken the advice of Flannery O'Connor's Misfit to do as much meanness as he can. From the opening scene in *The Orchard Keeper*, in which Kenneth Rattner is shoplifting, to the murder of the Kid in a Texas outhouse, which is the final action of *Blood Meridian*, McCarthy has compiled a 1,491-page catalog of viciousness unequaled by any other author I have read. No paraphrase does justice to the original, but McCarthy's fiction is particularly difficult to recount or describe. The mention of a head severed, a skull broken, an eye gouged out, a corpse violated hardly hints at the intensity of such actions as they are rendered by McCarthy. His ear for dialogue and his eye for detail are the best; although he occasionally overwrites, his prose is sharp and charged with energy; although his structure is weak, his narrative sequences are filled with movement and stunning imagery. He writes like a fallen angel, lavishing on the most depraved of human actions his brilliant style, his consummate technique.

McCarthy's theme is survival or, more than that, the celebration of the strong and the clever who live at the expense of others by cruelty and deception. In his moral economy, the only virtue is the ability to endure. His vision is fragmented, but there is something healthy in it. That aspect of the world that he has chosen to explore is firmly rooted in reality. What he sees he sees clearly, and above all he still knows the proper question to ask. At the end of *Blood Meridian* the sole survivor of a large band of cutthroats is a hairless giant, a peerless fighter and self-taught scholar called the judge. Here is the final paragraph of the narrative. The scene is a Texas saloon.

> And they are dancing, the board floor slamming under the jackboots and the fiddlers grinning hideously over their canted pieces. Towering over them all is the judge and he is naked dancing, his small feet lively and quick and now in doubletime and bowing to the ladies, huge and pale and hairless, like an enormous infant. He never sleeps, he says. He says he'll never die. He bows to the fiddlers and sashays backwards and throws back his head and laughs deep in his throat and he is a great favorite, the judge. He wafts his hat and the lunar dome of his skull passes palely under the lamps and he swings about and takes possession of one of the fiddles and he pirouettes and makes a pass, two passes, dancing and fiddling at once. His feet are light and nimble. He never sleeps. He says that he will never die. He dances in light and in shadow and he is a great favorite. He never sleeps, the judge. He is dancing, dancing. He says he will never die.

I cannot resist mentioning two other works in which the image of the dance has been used in a religious context: T. S. Eliot's "Burnt Norton" and Charles Williams' *The Greater Trumps*. I do not mean to imply that McCarthy's image is comparable with those of Williams and Eliot or that good and evil coalesce in McCarthy's novel. But evil can exist only as a defect of the good. It is a reversal, a denial, a parody, but always it is a defect. For example, there is no way to understand what a lie is unless first we have a concept of the truth, of which a lie is a defect. If truth should cease to exist, then the idea of a lie would be meaningless and would die with the death of truth. We can destroy only what has been created; we can steal only what a moral system has declared to be the property of another. Because evil is dependent for its existence on its opposite, it always implies the opposite, which is good.

McCarthy's judge is a parody of God—he is naked, like the guiltless Adam on the day of creation; he is a great favorite; he never sleeps; he will never die. This parody must take seriously the idea of God or it has no significance. Thus it thrusts us into a world where the possibility of the transcendent is valid. Although approached from a different angle, it is the same world in which the characters of Flannery O'Connor live their lives. I prefer O'Connor's vision to that of McCarthy, but I prefer McCarthy's work to that of the legion of writers, southern and otherwise, who ignore the question of the existence of the sacred or who do not know that there is such a question to be asked. Even to reject God knowingly is to remain in touch with reality in all its dimensions.

It is well enough to say, as I have said, that in a world bereft of the sacred the writer must furnish the sense of piety that society once furnished for him. But this leaves writers who do not have such a sense in a lurch, and I have no notion of how they can pull themselves out of it. More to my point is the fate of those who include a sense of the sacred in their work and offer it to a world that in general does not share their vision. As we know, Flannery O'Connor shouted and drew in bold lines, but since her death an industry has arisen to prove that she was not a Christian writer. Those southern writers who are endowed with less talent than O'Connor, those who speak with a softer voice and draw in thinner lines, are mostly doomed to wander the world like latter-day Prufrocks, not refuted or even criticized, but ignored, dismissed by publisher and public alike with ironic but tolerant smiles as anachronisms, representatives of an age and a philosophy that have been invalidated by modern ontologies.

But where in this gloomy scheme, you might ask, do we fit Eudora Welty and Walker Percy and Elizabeth Spencer? It is not coincidence that they all were raised in Mississippi, which has remained southern as long or longer than any other state and which endowed them with the southern sense of the sacred. They have by right of birth what is no longer available. For them the problem is solved, but for those born in other places and in other times it remains. It is presumptuous for me to give anyone advice, but I must do so to be true to my topic. I think southern writers in exile from the spirit of the contemporary world should seek in their work the sacred at the expense of the South.

This seems to be heresy, particularly to those of us who have been raised on the work of the giants of the Southern Renascence and who have seen the South as the most fertile of all fields for literary endeavor. But with its sense of piety gone, the South of the renascence must be recreated, and there is a danger for our fiction in our seeking out details that are specifically southern. Writers of fiction begin with the concrete, not with the abstract. Faulkner began with what he saw and heard, with what his senses told him, and in the shaping of details and sequences, he discovered the southern piety that underlay them. My contention is that under present circumstances, with the sense of the sacred gone, the shaping of details that are specifically southern will lead the writer to think he has done what Faulkner did, but he will not have done so. Rather he will have created work similar to that of Bobbie Ann Mason, whose stories are southern all right but are bereft of piety and meaning. The only way to recreate a South hospitable to the production of great literature is to recapture the sacred. I think, paradoxically perhaps, that the best way to do this is to seek the transcendent outside the ambience of southern imagery, because the images of the South, familiar and beloved as they are, tempt us to believe that we have not lost our piety. I do not mean that we must stop writing about the South forever. But we are writing about it badly now. Whether we recognize it or not, our spiritual diaspora has begun. It can be stopped only with a rejuvenation of the spirit.

Andrew Lytle: The Mythmaker at Home

In 1942 I was a sophomore at Vanderbilt, enrolled in "Advanced Composition" under Donald Davidson. This was a pivotal year for me. It was the last year I would spend as a civilian until World War II was over. And it was the year of my introduction into the serious study of literature. I had read books when I was coming up, but not enough good ones, and those with not much understanding. I had listened to Edwin Mims lecture on poetry during my freshman year. But even so, I came into Mr. Davidson's class innocent of any understanding of literature in general and of fiction in particular. Mr. Davidson set about to remedy that.

He assigned a text called *Contemporary Southern Prose*, which contained essays and serious book reviews, both of which I read when I was told to do so, but best of all there was a collection of stories that included "Jericho, Jericho, Jericho." I remember the first time I read that story: the chair I was sitting in and how the light fell on the page and most of all how I was transported from my own life into the life of a dying old lady. "She opened her eyes." This is the first sentence in Andrew Lytle's story, and I did not recognize then the wonder of its simplicity, the manner in which it immediately engages the reader with the narrative. Only after I had studied under Andrew, listened to him explain the virtues of the initial sentences of "The Open Boat," did I know enough properly to appreciate his own accomplishment. Even so, when I had finished my first reading of "Jericho" I knew what I had only suspected before: I wanted to spend my life reading literature and talking about literature and writing it myself, if I could. I do not say that Andrew is solely responsible for my misspent life. There is blame enough to go around, but he must take some of it.

After "Jericho" I read *At the Moon's Inn*, which was what I could find in the library. I read all one day and part of the night, and for the rest of the night I moved with de Soto in my dreams through the landscape that Andrew had described, enduring the hardships that Andrew had chronicled. By now I knew that a novel that could command your psyche in the way *At the Moon's Inn* commanded mine had to be a good book, though still I could not have said why. At this point my efforts at literary study were interrupted. I went into the Marine Corps and did not encounter Andrew's work again until the war was over and I was stationed at Marine Barracks in Washington, D.C., waiting to be discharged. Somebody with more enterprise than I had found his way to the post library— I never did discover where it was—and had brought back to the bachelor officers' quarters a copy of *The Long Night*. It was weakened from much handling, and many of its previous readers had left critical comments on the fly leaf: "Good" and "Very good" and "Excellent." However decrepit the physical book was, the *book*, the *real* book, was fully intact; it was Andrew again, weaving his spell, and it helped bring me from the world of the military back to that other world into which Andrew had helped lure me in the first place.

I first met Andrew Lytle in 1947 or 1948 under dour circumstances. We were at the University of Iowa in Iowa City. Housing was poor, the climate was bad, the people seemed alien, and I was not one of his best students. I had recently been married, and when I went to his office to discuss one of my manuscripts, Andrew told me that it was an old Jewish custom for men to take off their first year of marriage, on the theory that they would not be much good for anything until accustomed to their new domestic situation. I never knew whether this was true or whether he made it up to suit my circumstances, but I can testify that it was at once the kindest reprimand I ever received and the worst thing he ever said to me. As bad as I was, Andrew did not banish me. Not then. Not subsequently. For once you have become his student, you remain his student, and he continues to give you the most precious gifts he has in his possession: his affection, his advice, and his time.

Several years ago Madison Jones spent a summer at Monteagle, Tennessee. Madison's study overlooked Andrew's house, and Madison watched Andrew's visitors come and go, students and former students and would-be students, arriving early and staying late, availing themselves of Andrew's instructive company and Andrew's whiskey. As the summer wore on and the stream of visitors continued, Madison grew more and more restive. He himself had been a student of Andrew's and had in his day enjoyed a good deal of Lytle hospitality. But now Madison was a mature writer and knew the importance to a writer of time—not only time to write but time to think, to brood about what he did or did not get put on paper today and what problems might have to be faced tomorrow. His concern over Andrew's visitors, which I fully shared when we discussed the matter that summer, was not born solely out of his affection for Andrew. Madison and I believed that Andrew's work was too important to be interfered with. We wanted him left alone so he could produce more writing for us to read and to cherish. What we did not understand then was that without Andrew's generosity, his willingness to share himself with his friends, all the stories and books and essays that we loved would not have been quite the same. Andrew would have been a different person, and the work that he produced would have been different work.

Joseph Conrad said that "fiction appeals to temperament." More specifically it is "an appeal of one temperament to all the other innumerable temperaments" that will respond to what the writer with his individual temperament has written. I take this to mean, among other things, that the source of what a writer writes is his whole being: his mind to be sure, but also his heart; his beliefs, his values, all the large and small commitments of his life. Jacques Maritain apparently was thinking along these lines when he said, "Only a Christian, nay, a mystic, can be a complete novelist." The subject of fiction, Maritain went on, is "the conduct of human life itself," and only the mystic "has some idea of *what there is in man.*" Maritain refers here, I think, to our almost limitless capacities for good and for evil.

Although Conrad's comments on art continue to command respect, what Maritain had to say was not well received even by those who shared his theological position. François Mauriac, whose novels explore Christian themes, responded that Maritain was making novel writing a vocation for no one but saints; since novel writing is not one of the persecutions God ordinarily calls on his saints to endure, novelists who took Maritain literally might as well close up shop. But Mauriac went on writing. To my knowledge no other novelist bothered to respond to Maritain at all. Not many of them, I suspect, knew that he had said anything that needed answering.

No others responded, because art, as we understand it, is an invention of the modern age and therefore for most artists a secular endeavor. In *The Voices of Silence* André Malraux argues that we began to think of statues and paintings and cunningly wrought artifacts as art only after we had diverted them from their intended purposes and, in many cases, removed them from their proper locations. Crucifixes and holy pictures and figures of saints were created to be aids to the faithful in their worship, as were the statues of Greek and Roman and Egyptian deities. Portraits, whether done on canvas or in stone, were either part of a family's history or memorials to great events in the lives of cities or states. The holy picture was good to the degree that it created an atmosphere for fruitful worship; the bust of an ancestor or a soldier or a king was valuable to the degree that it kept public or private tradition alive and preserved and elucidated public or private history.

But consider what happens when the statue is taken from the temple, the crucifix is removed from the church, the ancestral portrait is lifted off the living room wall and all are gathered under one roof as part of a museum's collection. All these objects are given a new reason for being: They are no longer aids to worship or to memory, but works of art to be admired for themselves, for the brilliance with which they have been conceived and the skill with which they have been executed. They are to be perceived and experienced as things of beauty, and the experience of perceiving them is often profound. But they exist in a realm of their own: they have been segregated from the main thrust of human experience.

The history of literature is more complicated than that of the plastic arts. But as we move from ancient to modern times we see it turning away from the celebration of faith and nation and family to a new consciousness of literature as an end in itself and of the writer as a superior being not because of his moral qualities, but because of his aesthetic vision. In thinking this way, the writer embraces a shrunken concept both of himself and of the world in which he lives and about which he writes. The temperament of which Conrad spoke becomes distorted. Maritain's mystical quality, which enables the novelist to discover "what there is in man," is displaced by a mundane pursuit of literary technique. Any writer who sets out to stand against this spirit of the age must be prepared to endure slights and exclusions of both his work and himself. Only those with great strength and wisdom and a steady faith can stay the course. Andrew Lytle is one of them.

Around 1950 Andrew invited my wife Jane and me to visit him and his wife Edna at their farm in Robertson County. We arrived late on a summer afternoon, received the usual warm welcome, and settled down on the back veranda to drink out of the usual silver cups. Andrew was refurbishing his house: at the time he was laying a brick patio next to the porch where we were sitting. He discoursed on the joys and difficulties of farming. He had begun work on *The Velvet Horn*, which he was also willing to talk about, but only in those guarded terms that most writers employ when the project is still under way and the exploration of the theme remains unfinished.

This visit has assumed for me the dimensions of a parable. Behind us on the wall of the porch was an enormous Confederate flag. The Lytle children were fed their early supper in silver porringers. As the long twilight wore on, Andrew began to think of making a salad. "In a minute," he said, "we'll go to the woods and find some mushrooms." I was not rude enough to ask how we were going to distinguish the good mushrooms from the bad: I am certain that I did not raise the question. But Andrew has a finely tuned sense for the concerns of others, which is one of the foundations of his impeccable manners.

Andrew told Jane and me that there was no cause for concern. He had recently been studying mushrooms, and he had a book with excellent illustrations of both the good and the bad. He set out to reassure us, but his writer's sense of the dramatic would not be stifled. His attention was captured by those that could do us harm. One called the Destroying Angel—I am not certain of this name: it may have been the Avenging Angel, but it was some kind of angel and it was evil—was particularly hard to distinguish from one of the more succulent safe varieties with a safe, and therefore totally forgettable, name. The notion of this malevolent mushroom masquerading as a beneficent plant inspired Andrew's imagination. One of his great virtues as a writer and as a human being is that his mind never wanders far from the myth and the truth of our origins: our creation by God in his own image; our temptation and our fall. We have learned from Andrew's books that the drama played out among Eve and the Serpent and Adam in the Garden of Eden is played out over and over again in all our lives. That afternoon on his veranda Andrew suggested that the same theme is manifested in the vegetable world by the evil mushroom, decked out as was the Serpent in handsome apparel, waiting to do people harm. The ambiguity of the bad mushroom's name enhanced the situation and made it even more pleasant and profitable to contemplate.

Leaving for the moment what Cleanth Brooks has called, not unadmiringly, "Rutherford County metaphysics," Andrew turned from the moral symbolism of mushrooms to the comfort of his guests. He declared once more, modestly, that he knew mushrooms; but in the unlikely event that he made a mistake, there was a simple procedure to determine whether a mushroom were poisonous. Eat a piece the size of a dime. If you did not get sick within the next twelve hours, the mushroom was harmless; if you did get sick within the next twelve hours, the mushroom was toxic, but having eaten a piece no larger than a dime, you would not die. In thinking about the matter off and on for more than three decades, I have not yet figured out the logistics of this procedure as it applied to our circumstances. Putting aside the question of who was to eat the test piece of mushroom, what were we to do with the salad while waiting twelve hours to see if the tester got sick? I cannot answer this question, because the test was never made. We lingered so long over our cups that by the time Andrew had gotten his basket and we had walked to the woods, darkness had fallen. We ate a fine dinner with a good, but mushroomless, salad and talked far into the night.

The symbolism of this reminiscence is at once obvious and, for me at least, profound. The flag represents the past—tradition, of course, but not in any abstract sense: people, rather, real individuals who lived and fought and suffered and died and who remained, while they lived, willing to die for what they believed in. They were not all heroes; through the long generations before and after the Civil War each group was a mixed bag, but they are what we southerners come from. It is in terms of them, as Andrew has taught us, that we begin to define ourselves. Those well-behaved children, eating from their porringers, were the future—again no abstractions, but two little girls, to be taught, to be schooled in the ways of the past, so they could take with them into their own futures and for the benefit of children yet unborn, the best values and customs inherited from their ancestors.

The farm and the house on which Andrew was working with his own hands are significant because they are the antithesis of the modern technological, or as we say now, high-tech society. I need not dwell on the fact that technology, misused and misunderstood as we always seem to misuse and misunderstand it, is the enemy of individual integrity and of community. It tempts us to think that we *can* live by bread alone; it develops a myth of progress that induces us to believe in the perfectibility of human nature. Most of us deplore these tendencies in our lives, but as young Tarwater in Flannery O'Connor's novel says: "You can't just say No. . . . You got to do NO." Andrew was *doing* no. His life in his house and on his farm was a repudiation of what is worst about the modern age—its deceitful promises and its damaging fragmentations.

As for the mushrooms, Andrew was one of the few Agrarians who had lived the agrarian life; perhaps this is one reason that his contribution to *I'll Take My Stand* is thought by many critics to be the best of the twelve essays. Much of *The Long Night* was written not in a house but in the woods. Andrew could go confidently to search for mushrooms because he was and is at home with nature, which is to say with the mysteries of creation. God said, "Let there be light," and there was light. God said, "Let there be a firmament," and there was a firmament. God said, "Let there be man," and there was man. And somewhere down the line, God created mushrooms. The mystical sense of which Maritain speaks consists of being always aware, as Andrew is, that God created heaven and earth and all things therein and that all created things were good until man started to tamper with them. Anyone who has conversed seriously with Andrew has heard him speak of the Puritan heresy that manifests itself in the discovery of evil in the object rather than in the person who misuses the object; and of the mysterious and ultimately unfathomable connection between the Word made flesh and the words that are the incarnations of thought and the raw material of writers. His profound consideration of such themes is a source of his dignity as a man and his success as a novelist.

William Faulkner said that in order to do his work, a writer would and should steal from his grandmother. The "Ode on a Grecian Urn," he claimed, is worth more than any number of gray-haired old ladies. Whether or not Faulkner meant what he said, he was stating a principle familiar to twentieth-century writers: art, now long since removed from cathedral and home, has become deified. We are taught to revere it for itself alone and to make all other considerations subordinate to it. The private devotion to family represented by the grandmother must submit to the greater claims of the public act of presenting to the world the poem or novel or painting. The only private responsibility that the modern artist respects is his own act of creation. Thus an enmity is established between public and private loyalties that distorts the terms under which we ought to live and according to which art should be made.

From the start of his career, Andrew understood this. In Bedford Forrest he discovered a hero whose fidelity to family was unvitiated by his service to the state. *The Long Night* explores the conflicting claims of public and private devotion, and this theme is never far from his work. Finally, in *A Wake for the Living*, he refutes the notion of robbing one's grandmother for the sake of art by putting his own grandmother, as well as his aunts and uncles and cousins, into a book. They and his affection for them become part of his art, not enemies of it. They help him to define himself and his view of the human condition, a view that is broad and profound and that shall continue to enrich us for as long as we read his work. Andrew Lytle sees the world whole, but his vision begins with home and family—on a porch in Robertson County, Tennessee, or by the fire in the log cabin at Monteagle, or wherever those who love him can draw near.

Part II

Irony and Disorder: *The Secret Agent*

Like much of Joseph Conrad's work, *The Secret Agent* has both its warm admirers and its vehement detractors. But all who comment on it speak of the tone, the ironic voice with which Conrad tells his story, of the contending forces of order and disorder, and of the interplay of public and private image, political and domestic conflict, which culminate in the murder of Adolf Verloc and the suicide of his wife. Whatever we think of the novel, however we intend ultimately to interpret it, we cannot avoid going so far as this together, for up to this point Conrad tells us what was in his mind. We know that he came to the material for *The Secret Agent* after two years of intense absorption, first with *Nostromo* and later with *Mirror of the Sea*. He talked with Ford Madox Ford about the by then not-so-recent attempt to destroy the Greenwich observatory, he read a memoir by an assistant commissioner of police, and at last he turned his attention to two of his own images. One was the city, vast and impersonal and all-encompassing; the other was Winnie Verloc, strictly circumscribed, withdrawn, myopic, and, until the book's violent ending, a relatively passive presence. Between these poles the other characters and events arranged themselves; the ironic treatment makes Conrad's skeptical attitude toward the whole business abundantly clear.

Indeed the method of irony is so deeply established in the novel, the sometimes comic objectivity so unrelenting in its working over people and events, that the tone merges with and becomes theme, suggesting to us ways of interpretation. For example, we are shown so clearly Verloc's alienation on every level of his existence, his increasing loss of identity, his abandonment of national and familial loyalties, that we are likely to see him as more representative of our own time than of Conrad's. He is in some respects the quintessential modern man, and with a little cleverness we can comprehend his role as that of the hero in a sort of modern tragedy. Having set out on a course of revolutionary endeavor, Verloc is seduced from his stance by his desire for ease and his own slothful nature. Unwilling either to live in poverty or to work, he becomes a double agent, reporting—though as little as possible—on his colleagues-in-revolution, who are the only friends he has. His fear of losing his regular paycheck from the Russian embassy leads to the abortive attempt to destroy the observatory, to the death of Stevie, and ultimately to the wretched ends of both Verloc and his wife.

When we bring Mrs. Verloc into our consideration, the delineations of the tragic tale become Hegelian. As in *Antigone*, but with its own special tawdriness, *The Secret Agent* brings into conflict the claims of family, represented by Winnie Verloc's devotion to her brother, and the larger demands of an organized state. The consequences of this contention are again the deaths of the various parties involved, but of course there is no real resolution and certainly no reaffirmation. We do not leave the book with a sense of hope, but with an image of the Professor imprinted on our minds—this madman loose in the world, with a flask of nitroglycerin in his coat and his hand on the detonator. What we have witnessed is not tragedy at all, but an antitragedy, an aping of the old forms and standards. As I have suggested, Verloc is a man without values and without fidelities or commitments except to himself. Mrs. Verloc, who carries in the novel the burden of domestic virtue, has from the beginning violated the nature of the marriage sacrament: she has married not for love but for her brother's security. Her murder of Verloc in vengeance for the at least partially accidental death of her brother indicates the distorted affections on which her whole relationship with Verloc has been founded. The disintegration at the end of the novel violates all vestiges of good in the contending forces and rends rather than heals the ethical substance of the universe.

The Verlocs, in their moral deviations, set a pattern of attitude and conduct for the other characters in the book. That the world and its people once were more orderly is suggested by Chief Inspector Heat, who, in an oft-cited passage, longs for the good old days, when policemen pursued honest criminals who themselves had a stake in the established working of things. If the bank robber were to thrive, then banks must exist for him to rob, and here his interest in a stable society coincided with those of the government and the police representing it. All acknowledged the same set of rules, under which by common consent some were innocent and some were culpable. As Heat perhaps imperfectly understands, when the system is abrogated, the entire social fabric is damaged and finally each person is reduced to his own moral resources.

This is another way of saying that in our secular society, anarchy leads to situation ethics, to each doing his own will, usually in innocence of his own essential nature. A minor but revealing figure in *The Secret Agent* is the old dowager Annie, patroness of the anarchist and paroled convict Michaelis, and of others like him, and espouser of revolutionary causes. She is rich and well-born, and in her confusion she mistakes the genetic accident that has elevated her economically and socially as evidence of natural superiority and even sanctity. She sees herself as perfect and enduring, incapable of error, immune from the violence and vicissitudes of private accident or public upheaval. She believes that she is above life— its ebb and flow, its causes and consequences—and therefore she can do as she pleases. Since she will remain forever untouched, all eventualities of whatever sort are for her mere abstractions.

All the characters in the book echo in their own ways Annie's grand selfishness. The other revolutionaries are no better than Verloc. They are lazy and ineffectual at best, and for the most part they are untrustworthy even in their intercourse with one another. Of Yundt we are told:

> The famous terrorist had never in his life personally raised as much as his little finger against the social edifice. . . . He was no man of action. . . . With a more subtle intention, he took the part of an insolent and venomous evoker of sinister impulses which lurk in the blind envy and exasperated vanity of ignorance, in the suffering and misery of poverty, in all the hopeful and noble illusions of righteous anger, pity and revolt. The shadow of his evil gift clung to him yet like the smell of a deadly drug in an old vial of poison.

Michaelis, his natural inclination toward the abstract exacerbated by his long stay in prison, lives wrapped within himself, his corpulence a symbol of his isolation from the realities of life. The lecherous Ossipon deceives Mrs. Verloc in her hour of need, taking her money and abandoning her to self-destruction.

Among those on the other side, the representatives of organized society, a similar moral ambiguity prevails. Mr. Vladimir of the Russian embassy is a contemptible figure, a famous wit and habitué of drawing rooms whose ethic is completely Machiavellian. He suggests the assault on order—the destruction of the observatory for what he believes to be the sake of preserving the status quo. But the end he seeks is as deeply flawed as the means he would employ; his only ideal is to keep himself in power. The English are better—as they or the French or anybody else is always better than the Russians in Conrad's fiction—but they are not good enough, for Chief Inspector Heat in his way is a less brutal and more public-spirited version of Vladimir.

Like Vladimir, Heat knows that his own interests are best served when he does his job well, and like Vladimir's, his job is to defend what is. The difference is that Heat represents a democratic government and Vladimir is part of a viciously repressive system. The significance of this distinction is that Vladimir will initiate evil, while Heat will only take advantage of it; but once they have set forth on their missions they operate in the same general way. Vladimir will destroy the observatory in an effort to have England pass stricter laws governing subversives. Once the bomb has gone off, Heat will use the outrage as an excuse to round up the same subversives, not because he believes them guilty of this particular crime, but because he recognizes here a chance to get them off the streets. And the Assistant Commissioner, though more refined still, is nonetheless culpable.

Certainly we can believe that the Assistant Commissioner is absolutely honest in his determination to protect Michaelis and others like him from unjust arrest. But no motive is unmixed or arrived at outside the context of self-interest. The Assistant Commissioner's wife is a friend of the socially powerful Annie, who is Michaelis' patron, and like any other man the Assistant Commissioner cherishes domestic harmony. Beyond this, in fulfilling his professional role he acts out of pique and naïveté. Having been transferred from a foreign post that suited him, he does not like his current position, and he rightly feels that Heat views him with distrust tinged with animosity. But most remarkable of all is his inability or his unwillingness to see the world as it is. He regards Heat's system of informers, developed by great effort and patience and of considerable value to the work of the police, as fundamental duplicity. It is, of course, but it is also a means of protecting the innocent, and when the Assistant Commissioner destroys it, he leaves nothing in its place.

Finally there is Winnie Verloc's mother, who is absolutely that, the mother circumscribed, cut off by her fierce maternal devotion from all external conflicts or considerations. Her single ambition is to guarantee a continuing home for Stevie; to achieve that end, she commits herself to an almshouse. Her excruciating trip across London displays a seldom-noted aspect of Conrad's genius. As others have pointed out, the scene is almost Dickensian in its development and trappings: the ruined carriage, the disfigured coachman, the starving horse. The two women and the idiot boy bounce over the cobbles in an agony of love and self-sacrifice and misunderstanding. Their voices are muted, and their understatements are emphasized by the physical images surrounding them: the dark and decaying city and the foggy night.

The deprivation that Mrs. Verloc's mother embraces, the mother's sacrifice, evolves from motives undeniably pure. She is going, Conrad tells us, "to a charity cottage . . . which by the exiguity of its dimensions and the simplicity of its accommodations might well have been devised in kindness as a place of training for the still more straitened circumstances of the grave." But the mother's motives are too severely limited, too careless of all claims on the future except Stevie's happiness. She disappears into her asylum, there, we assume, to die a natural death and perhaps never to know of the violent destruction of her family. But her single-minded devotion to her son has made nothing change.

It is instructive to see what, at the end of the book, remains the same and what is altered. The main parties are dead. Ossipon's nerves have been shattered by Mrs. Verloc's suicide, for which he cannot evade responsibility. The Russian ambassador is discredited. Heat's old police methods have been rendered at least temporarily useless, the Assistant Commissioner winning a victory of sorts. But Annie goes on untouched and impervious, her drawing room open and her protection available to whatever idea or personality attracts her fancy. The Professor goes on, carrying with him through the streets and into the company of innocent people not only his explosive flask, but also his almost palpable anger and his terrifying will to destroy. And the government goes on (or so we think), immune (we think) to whatever small upheavals separate and claim the lives of individual men.

Obviously this book speaks more clearly and more frighteningly to us than it could have spoken to its first readers in 1907. The Annies among us have multiplied, financing the Professors who have increased a thousand-fold; as the bombs go off with appalling regularity, the survival of our institutions and even of the order of time and space represented by the Greenwich observatory no longer appears to be guaranteed. *The Secret Agent* contains in extraordinarily large measure a warning against the perils that we now face. But simply to predict the future, to show us our follies in their political and social delineations, is not enough. Literature, to be literature, must be timeless. It must—at least some of us still think—probe the unchanging moral questions that plague and define us as human beings, generation after generation. And more than this it must have a metaphysical dimension. As William F. Lynch has said, we must go through the finite to the infinite. Or, as Conrad himself put it in that most famous of all his critical musings, we must tell the sensuous truth first—make the reader hear and feel and see—and the larger verities will follow.

This is part of the magic of literature: the expanding image, the way that character and event transcend the limitations of the space and time in which they have their genesis. Verloc and his cohorts, as well as Heat and his, are first of all men of their own age; as such they prefigure our own agonies. But in his skillful rendition of them and in his attitude toward them—which is to say, in the tone he established for his narrative—Conrad makes them into avatars of the human condition. What they show us is our inability to stand alone, to solve our own problems, to survive by a mere dependence on our own cerebral processes.

Conrad was not in the ordinary way a pious man. As Graham Greene has pointed out, his religious impulse was founded on "little more than a distant memory of the Sanctus bell and the incense. Conrad was born a Catholic and ended—formally—in consecrated ground, but all he retained of Catholicism was the ironic sense of an omniscience and of the final unimportance of human life under the watching eyes." I will add one thing more: he kept to the doctrine of original sin. He never allowed himself to be deceived concerning the true nature of humankind. Therefore tone—which is a manifestation of the artist's way of seeing, a product of the individual artistic temperament in reaction to and with and against the material—tone, particularly in this work by Conrad, becomes and functions as theme. As much as the characters and the plot, the language itself—reflecting as it does Conrad's ironic view of human endeavor, his certainty that things will be botched in the end, his doubts about all our fine dreams and our tainted procedures—conveys the absurdity of the world as Conrad saw it and the moral frailty of those who inhabit it.

A Sense of Place: Elizabeth Bowen and the Landscape of the Heart

At the end of her career Elizabeth Bowen's work was in a state of decline. Like a baseball pitcher who starts aiming for the plate, Bowen in her closing years was trying to achieve by main force the drama and ambiguity and profundity that accrued naturally to her work in her finest days. *A World of Love* was a shadow, an anemic imitation of the best of her novels, and *The Little Girls* and *Eva Trout* were *tours de force* that did not succeed. Although she had completed less than ten pages of the novel she was writing when cancer overtook her in 1973, it seems safe to say that this too would have been a failure under the standards established in her early major fiction. So from a literary point of view our regret at her going must center on the fact that her autobiography remained largely unwritten when she died. The fragment of the novel and the two completed chapters of the autobiography were included in a volume collected by Spencer Curtis Brown in 1975. Victoria Glendinning's affectionate life of Bowen, published in 1978, is valuable for the facts it contains, but our knowledge of the heart and mind of Elizabeth Bowen must still come mostly from her work.

Elizabeth Dorothea Cole Bowen was one of that strange if not unique breed—the Anglo-Irish. Protestants among Catholics, landholders among tenants, loyalists among rebels, they remained somehow Irish in spite of their fidelity to the English crown. Although she was later to inherit the ancestral estate in County Cork, she was born in Dublin because her father had quarreled with his father and removed himself from Bowen's Court. Indeed, even among the Irish the Bowens, who were originally Welsh, were known for their general irascibility and for a strain of mental weakness, which took Henry Bowen to an institution and Elizabeth and her mother to England when Elizabeth was seven years old. Here, Bowen tells us, her career as a novelist unconsciously began. Filled with love for Ireland and its culture, she found herself, not unhappily, in a distinctly strange milieu. Shuttled from one relative to another, moved from school to school, she observed the curious ways of the English and developed a strong attachment to the slant of English sunlight and the lie of English land.

According to her own testimony her fictional process, the manner of her creating, always started with place. Other novelists might begin with a concept of character or with a germ of a story or with a human situation that they feel compelled to probe. But with Elizabeth Bowen there was first the deliberate limning of the landscape or the drawing room or the street or the park. Of all the places that she described, houses were obviously her favorites. Think of Anna's house in *The Death of the Heart*, of the house in Paris that gives one novel its title, and of Stella's flat with its curtains to seal in the air and the light in *The Heat of the Day*. Although her characters move about—there are sequences that take place in Ireland and England in *The House in Paris*—it is impossible to read Bowen and not be aware of how architecture and topography give weight to her fiction and contribute actively to the development of plot and theme.

The estate in *The Last September* is not only the center of the action but a symbol of what the action is about. The house, patterned obviously after Bowen's Court, is the locus of the main characters, the Naylors and the Montmorencys and Lois, and of Marda Naylor. From here the grounds reach out and the action follows: to the tennis courts, along the shadowed driveway, down the stream where Hugo conducts his illicit pursuit of Marda, to the building where Marda and Lois find the armed man. Even when the plot of the narrative takes us to the army barracks or to the nearby city, the presence of Danielstown encroaches on the action, representing as it does the troubles of that time.

The static quality of Mme. Fisher's bedroom in *The House in Paris*, as Bowen herself pointed out, exerts a kinetic force on the characters in the book. The chamber and its dying occupant are the stillness at the center, the heart of the story without which nothing else could take place. Speaking from her station beneath the covers, Mme. Fisher gives us our first hint of Max's infidelity, of Miss Fisher's unhappiness, of poor Leopold's impending disappointment and generally precarious position in life. Even in the long flashback composing the second section of the novel, the houses in Ireland and England keep the house in Paris fresh in one's memory, and the melancholy illness of Aunt Violet is a counterpoint to Miss Fisher's moribund state.

In *The Death of the Heart* Thomas' study is balanced against the perfection of Anna's drawing room, and Matchett's downstairs quarters radiate warmth in contrast to those precincts that are under Anna's hegemony. Each bedroom has its own quality, and the house at Seale-on-Sea, where Portia visits the Heccombs, is delineated by the implied comparison with the more stately edifices at Regent's Park. I would hesitate to continue along this line except that Bowen has invited us or, more, has insisted that we do so. The decaying house at the beach, the paint cracked, the shutters flapping, is a proper setting for Eddie to continue his betrayal of Portia, and the house in turn becomes symbolic of the action it enfolds. More subtly the hotel where Major Brutt lives reflects not only his honest poverty, but the fact that with all his simple probity he, like the building, has fallen behind the times.

The Heat of the Day is a slightly different matter, for the damages of war are not to be avoided; ruins, like ghosts or corpses, carry their own power and set their own mood. But of course Elizabeth Bowen knew this, and what she attains in this otherwise flawed novel is the sense of places yet unexploded; we see their wholeness as a reflection of the encompassing threat. I have already mentioned Stella's sealed apartments, at one of which Robert is killed. Holme Dene is malignant in its ugliness and isolation; Wistaria Lodge shares the uncertainty of the demented people it shelters; with its eternally chilled drawing room, Mount Morris broods over past evils, a tradition irretrievably fading, and a future shrouded in gloom.

Because Elizabeth Bowen was a novelist of manners, a principal problem for the reader is to discover the public dimension in the author's work. In *The Last September*, which in my judgment is the first of her major novels, the solution is conventional. Like the people in the time of Noah who continue eating and drinking and giving in marriage to the end, the characters at Danielstown go their ways, generally indifferent to the gathering clouds, though the clouds are undeniably, palpably there. While the Naylors and their guests are walking in the garden, taking tea in the dining room, and assembling for tennis parties and dances, the characters warn one another against walks in the darkness and daylight dangers on lonely roads. The IRA works at its purpose, the British soldiers do their duty; armored trucks move along the highway, armed men stand at milestones; offstage, raids are conducted and people die.

In our present climate of seeing everything in such colors, it would be easy to comprehend this novel in political terms. Some critics have done so, but this approach misses the point. If Elizabeth Bowen had any misgivings concerning her family's role in Irish history, she kept them carefully hidden; never did they emerge to affect her work. But like all good novelists of manners, she was aware that small actions are reflections of a larger context; events in the drawing room mirror those in Parliament and courtroom and cathedral.

Thus the apparent stability of the Naylors and the uncertainty of the Montmorencys combine to make an image of the contradictions of the human state in general and of this particular time and place. Laurence's deficiency of purpose and unconcern for his future, Marda's indifference toward the man she is going to marry, Francie's spiritual and physical debilities all imply dislocations on a larger scale.

The thematic climax, coming early in the novel, is likely to pass unrecognized until the final page is read. In an effort to escape the married Hugo's advances, the soon-to-be-married Marda, joined by Lois, takes refuge in a ruined mill. The girls come upon a sleeping rebel, whose gun discharges accidentally and slightly injures Marda's hand. This is strong action for Bowen, more violence than she allows herself in her later novels; but all the elements of the story come together here and reverberate outward with the sound waves from the shot. The characters with their strengths and weaknesses fall into place, and their roles are illuminated. "I must marry Gerald," Lois tells herself while the desperate man points his pistol at her. She will not marry Gerald, for that would bring her into a fuller recognition of the dimensions of human reality; and she, like the other characters, like most of the rest of mankind, is not ready for that. Mesmerized by the present, Lois cannot accept Gerald's proposal and thereby perhaps save his life any more than the Naylors can awaken themselves to danger in time to save Danielstown or the Montmorencys can carry through any of their plans.

The Last September is exquisitely of a piece; every nuance of the denouement is totally prepared for; nothing is taken for granted or left to chance. Bowen was to do even better. *The Death of the Heart* is generally thought to be her masterpiece, and I make no cavil at this judgment, but *The House in Paris* is almost as fine. The superiority of *The Death of the Heart* results perhaps from the fullness of Portia's characterization and from the novel's larger scope. But much of the restriction that *The House in Paris* suffers from in the narrowness of its boundaries is offset by the tightness of its structure and the dramatic intensity of its scenes. I have mentioned already Bowen's own admiration for her achievement with Mme. Fisher—how the sick old lady controls, without moving from her bed, the present events of the book by the force of her will. The people in this novel are drawn well, as they always are in Bowen's work, and the love affair between Karen and Max is absolutely convincing.

Here again one is reminded of Elizabeth Bowen's use of place. The cold and rainy seaside, the cheerless room where the affair is consummated, the church bells, the people who pass in pursuit of more respectable enterprises all add substance and truth to the relationship of the lovers. So it is when they meet in France. In the background of the story there is no war: no gunshots or conflagrations testify to the existence of the larger world. Still the private act is never private. Society marks its own reality by the intricacies of human relationships—the broken heart of Miss Fisher and the loneliness and insecurity of Leopold—and by the deaths of those whose agonies have become too great—Karen's mother, an innocent victim, and Max, who in his guilt chooses death.

At the beginning and end of this novel are touches that show Elizabeth Bowen at her particular best. Henrietta, child and female, utterly ignorant but intuitively wise, breaks by her presence one of fiction's traditional conventions: she is an extra character; she has no stake in the action; what happens to Leopold and the others is none of her affair. Yet she is the first character we meet, and her humane concern for the dispossessed Leopold is our concern and the world's concern. More than anyone else she endows the book with its breadth and depth; on her own small shoulders she bears the burden of doing for *The House in Paris* what was done for *The Last September* by the war.

Finally there is Ray. Until he appears at the Fisher house as Karen's surrogate, he has been only a name, a personage heard of in the story but not yet seen. He too is evidence that individual actions not only have consequences but also assert the morality of the tribe. He has been injured in both the formal and the most personal senses of that word. Embarrassed and hurt by Karen's betrayal of him, he arrives at the house to make amends for Karen's faithlessness, sensing perhaps an identity with Leopold in the compromised roles they both fill. Yet Bowen will not oversimplify; the attachment between Leopold and Ray will not be easy. It may not in the long run even be possible. But Ray's effort, at the conclusion of the novel, completes the frame set at the beginning by Henrietta; his presence supports hers in making the book something more than the simple love story it might otherwise have been.

Leopold, the lost and suffering center of *The House in Paris*, foreshadows the more richly drawn Portia in *The Death of the Heart*. She is surely Bowen's finest creation. Like Leopold she is the offspring of an irregular arrangement, and we take up her story where his ends. After a life lived in hotels at the very edge of respectability, she is sent at her mother's death to stay with her half-brother and his wife at Regent's Park. At once knowing and innocent, well-mannered but socially naïve, she becomes for Anna an annoyance and an enigma, for Portia's goodwill and honesty have neither value nor currency in Anna's fashionable world. A lesser novelist than Bowen might have been content to make of this a mere adversary relationship, the conflict between innocence and sophistication, maturity and youth. But the lines in *The Death of the Heart* are by no means so clearly drawn.

With her way of telling the truth whatever the circumstances, of trusting the untrustworthy, and of loving the unlovable, Portia by her presence is bound to introduce problems into any civilized house. As Flannery O'Connor liked to point out, we are sufficiently at home with the flaws of mankind to be able to cope with them. But few of us are prepared for a direct confrontation with the good. Anna's intentions are impeccable; she wants to do well by Portia just as she wants to help Major Brutt find a job, but in both cases her efforts are frustrated by their inability to play her kind of game. Their social ignorance is their moral strength: they meet every turn with absolute candor; in all their actions they refuse to dissemble; when they move or speak they are likely to damage themselves.

Eddie, as is proper for the villain of such a novel, is sketched with more complicated lines. He intends to accomplish not so much ill for others as good for himself. His vindictiveness, apparent in the book he has written and in his cruelty to Portia, is an aspect of his selfishness. His obsequious attentions to Anna, his courtship of Daphne, his slothfulness, and his extravagance all proceed from his determination to set himself right in his own eyes and in those of his friends. His visit to Seale-on-Sea is a disaster because he cannot decide what part he ought to assume. Afraid of what the younger Heccombs might think of him, he withdraws from Portia's love, driving her to tears with harsh words of rejection, gets drunk, and leaves a day early. He is belligerent to hide his inner weakness; his effrontery—making free with the office telephone, visiting Anna without invitation—is a manifestation of his fear. Whatever his motives, his disordered behavior works to the disadvantage of others; Portia is particularly vulnerable because she longs for him to be better than he is.

Portia, doomed by goodness, is not to be spared. She is an existential character in the best sense of the term. She pursues meaning in an imperfect world; she pits her own goodness against the evils and agonies of the human condition in an effort to cope with life on her own terms and according to her own moral precepts. But to deal effectively with life is to compromise, and this she cannot bring herself to do. Since she will not negotiate her principles, how are Anna and Thomas and Mrs. Heccomb and even Eddie to deal with her? In her stiff rectitude she is too loyal to Eddie, too subservient—

though in an unconsciously ironic way—to Daphne, too se-
cretive with Anna, too open in the entries in her diary. Her
pure innocence, admirable as it is, is a kind of excess and an
extravagance of virtue that impedes the normal course of life.
Thus the conclusion of the novel can offer no solution. By
retreating to Major Brutt, that lost and feckless but good man,
Portia stands firm. This symbolic escape constitutes a sort of
victory. But on the last page Matchett has come to fetch her
back to the old confrontation, the old pain.

The Heat of the Day presented Elizabeth Bowen with new
fictional problems, which she did not fully solve. For one
thing she was attempting to work on a more public if not a
larger scale. The novel takes place in London during World
War II; the basic plot is built around Stella Rodney's discovery
that her lover is a traitor to his country, a Nazi spy. This kind
of material involved Bowen in the sort of thing that she was
least fitted for, discussions of ideologies and questions of political right and wrong. Because of the historical context she
was forced to start with the general—wartime London, global
conflict, competing moral philosophies—and work toward
the particular—Stella's love for Robert and Harrison's pursuit
of them, Louie's casual pregnancy, Rodney's assumption of
the burdens of family continuity and fidelity to the past.

The characters are delineated well by ordinary standards,
but they are not so good as those in Bowen's earlier fiction.
Some of her English critics, who lived through the enveloping
action of the novel, were pleased with the author's evocation
of atmosphere, the spirit of wartime England. But this world,
however accurately depicted, is not Elizabeth Bowen's world;
and the society, the organization of Western culture that supported and informed her best efforts, was not to be found
again in her lifetime. The symbolic destruction that she had
devised for the ending of *The Last September* was repeated by
the Nazi bombers that destroyed the houses at Regent's Park.
With them, in the playing out of our recent history, went all
the certainties that undergirded Bowen's work. Established

conventions ceased to be. Moral absolutes decayed. Without a society to support them or a transcendent authority to which to appeal, the passage of dialogue and the gesture in the drawing room ceased to signify more than themselves. Words remained simply words spoken; the surreptitious hand upon the thigh came to mean no more than the flicking of ash from a cigarette.

Elizabeth Bowen responded to the changed circumstances of the world in ways that should have been predictable because they were so singularly her own. In 1952 she attempted to take up life at Bowen's Court. But when her husband died she was forced to sell the estate; thus Ireland and family and the rich complexities of the past were denied her. So, like some of her distinguished contemporaries, she turned to Rome, but in her own fashion: she remained an Anglican and took herself physically to the Holy City. It was simply in her to begin with places, and there were architecture and space enough in Rome to soothe her heart's pain and to satisfy its yearning. Here the buildings, the fountains, the statues helped to liberate her from what she called "the thicket of self." She left Rome with tears in her eyes, rejuvenated and renewed in her faith. She would live another fourteen years, but her career as a major novelist was over.

Waugh Revisited

As everyone knows, Evelyn Waugh himself, the persona, was an embarrassment to the English-speaking literary community, which bridled at his politics and snickered at his religion. His existence as a novelist was certified only because in much of his early work he satirized the upper classes. Then came *Brideshead Revisited* (1945), which celebrates Catholicism and the English aristocracy, and Waugh became and remains to this day an object of scorn for many intellectuals. As most critics claim, *Brideshead* is a pivotal novel; although Waugh seems to revert to his earlier orientation in such works as *The Loved One* (1948), after publication of *Brideshead* he was essentially a Catholic novelist.

Waugh's basic method in his early work and in all of his comic writing was to use the old device of having his characters respond to situations in ways that shocked and often offended conventional expectations: in *Decline and Fall* (1928) Lady Circumference's fear that the death of her son and not her desire to snub the hostess will be taken as the reason she does not attend a party; in *Vile Bodies* (1930) Nina's reply—"Oh, *Adam*, you are a bore"—when he tells her he must break their engagement; in *A Handful of Dust* (1934) the complacency of the Hetton congregation when the rector, who once served in India, preaches a Christmas sermon about heat and tigers. Such scenes show how tone and humor work together for Waugh or, more accurately, how he used tone to generate humor. The comic effect thus produced is perhaps not an end in itself—black comedy for its own sake—but a means of getting through life, of fending off the sorrows of spirit and flesh that commonly afflict us.

It is also probably true that Waugh's interest in the upper classes does not result merely from the novelist's snobbery but rises as well from his recognition that, like the barbarous and the insane, the aristocracy are a law unto themselves. Hemingway's witty rejoinder notwithstanding, Fitzgerald was right about people with money. Freed from concern over the material demands of existence, they settle into codes of conduct based on a perception of reality that excludes anxieties over material things. Like mindless youths and savage kings and inmates of asylums, they surmount the vicissitudes of quotidian existence with the humorous line, the comic gesture. But such statements are not final, and such victories cannot last.

One question that intrigues many commentators on Waugh is why his Catholicism, which he embraced in 1930, did not become a factor in his fiction until fifteen years later. His travel books with their descriptions of churches and liturgies and comparisons of Eastern and Western rites make his new faith evident enough. But one looks in vain for the Catholic influence in *Black Mischief* (1932), *Scoop* (1938), *Put Out More Flags* (1942), and *Work Suspended* (1942). Nor will it do to see *A Handful of Dust* as an adumbration of Waugh's Catholic novels, though this line is taken by many critics. The argument goes that in this book Waugh dealt seriously with Tony's lack of faith and beyond this with the malaise afflicting the established church in England. But this is not a new element in Waugh's fiction. The mysterious Father Rothchild in *Vile Bodies* deplores the lack of religious feeling in the young; and, in any event, concern over a general decline in religious belief is not a uniquely Catholic response.

I say Catholic, not simply Christian, not something interchangeable with other denominations. In March, 1948,

Waugh wrote to Penelope Betjeman, who was soon to be confirmed a Catholic: "You are coming into the Church with vastly more knowledge than most converts but what you cannot know until Tuesday is the delight of membership of the Household, of having your chair at the table, a place laid, the bed turned down, of the love & trust, whatever their family bickerings, of all Christendom. It is this family unity which makes the weakest Catholic nearer the angels & saints, than the most earnest outsider."

Three years earlier, in *Brideshead*, Sebastian had put the case more strongly. Responding to Charles Ryder's observation that Catholics "seem just like other people," he replied, "That's exactly what they're not . . . they've got an entirely different outlook on life; everything they think important, is different from other people." This is true, and it is the reason that *Brideshead* is a hopeless muddle for many readers. To read Waugh without some understanding of the Catholic impulse that shapes his late fiction is like trying to read Faulkner with no knowledge of the South.

Most rationalists, being people of goodwill, are willing to suspend their disbelief in favor of a work of literature cast in a Christian ambience. The mythology of virgin birth, miracles performed, crucifixion, and resurrection are acceptable as a dramatic frame; the Christian messages of love and brotherhood and sacrifice for others are easily understood and admirable. Thus the confused but kind and well-meaning Scobie in Graham Greene's *The Heart of the Matter* is deemed a proper literary hero. But think of Francis of Assisi, perhaps among the world at large the most widely known of all Catholic saints outside the Virgin Mary and the Apostles. He is greatly admired for his way with the birds and for moving a worm out of the road. But how many of us can comprehend that the most profound fulfillment of his life was brought about by the wounds on his hands and feet, the stigmata? To speak of a love so strong that it yearns to participate in the suffering of the Beloved is well and good. But what is accomplished by these bleeding sores that do not feed the poor or cure the sick or make life easier for a single human being? Nothing, of course, in the mundane sense. They must be evaluated in terms of a transcendent economy.

I do not say that this is an economy that all Catholics understand or that it is one that is inexorably closed to Protestant comprehension. Among Anglicans there are T. S. Eliot and C. S. Lewis and Dorothy Sayers, to name but three, who would have totally sympathized with Bridey Marchmain's thought concerning the relationship of this world to the next; but beyond question Waugh's absolutist views of church and state cost him the sympathy of major segments of society at large and earned him the bitter enmity of most intellectuals. After Vatican II he was out of step with the leaders of his own faith. He called for a return to the Tridentine Mass; he declared his admiration for Saint Pius V—who had excommunicated Elizabeth I—even as John XXIII sought closer relationships with other religious and secular groups in an effort to bring Catholic thought into the mainstream of world affairs.

The difficulty we encounter in assessing Waugh's work is compounded by this stubborn conservatism. We ask too much of critics if we expect them to be purely objective. Recent developments in critical theory and literary practice notwithstanding, literature and the discussion thereof are intellectual arts. What the writer says does matter, even if we try to believe and to behave as if it does not. But since we do not like to admit this or to admit that we might be prejudiced by our disagreement with an author, we castigate Waugh for the romanticism of *Brideshead*, when we are equally offended by the Catholic obsession with eschatology and the Catholic value system that urges us to sacrifice happiness in the here and now for the promise of greater happiness beyond the grave.

The charges made against *Brideshead* are too numerous fully to discuss here. Waugh seemed to agree that the book was overwritten, or at least too much of a good thing: between the first and subsequent trade editions, he cut some of the more elegant passages. It is true that Sebastian, who with Charles is a principal figure in the first half of the book, fades from the narrative to be replaced by Julia. But to fault the structure of the novel on this ground is to take a Procrustean view that disallows a unity based on the development of theme. More serious flaws, according to most critics, are Lord Marchmain's deathbed repentance and Julia's sudden decision to honor her Catholic upbringing and adhere to Catholic marriage laws.

That there are daily deathbed conversions and reconversions is of little help. The kind of fiction Waugh wrote demands not simply that fictional events be possible in terms of actual human existence but that they be probable—and ideally inevitable—in terms of the fictions in which they appear. But faith is a gift, sanctity is a calling, and God, who gives and calls, works according to his own concept of form and is indifferent to criticism. Some basic tensions of Waugh's novel depend on Lord Marchmain's animus toward his wife and, through her, toward the Church. He is until his repentance an embodiment of the habits and values of the secular world. In defending his abandonment of his family, he pleads one of the major philosophical clichés of our time: he was, he declares, seeking his own freedom. Later, when life and infirmity have deprived him of carnal joys, he comforts himself with a proud recitation of aristocratic honors, the titles and position to which he has been heir.

With a little ingenuity Lord and Lady Marchmain can be perceived as allegorical figures. She is a suffering and self-sacrificing saint on the sure road to paradise; he is the uncharitable philanderer, enjoying like Dives his happiness on earth. To pursue this interpretation among the fine details of the novel would be extravagant; I wish only to delineate the dramatic tension to which I refer. Without Lord Marchmain's contribution to the moral chaos of the Flyte family, the novel would lose much of its force. Had Waugh attempted to adumbrate Lord Marchmain's repentance, he could have done so only by weakening Marchmain's role as defector from and antagonist to the faith. In the absence of such foreshadowing, only a Catholic commitment by his readers will save Waugh from the charge of having manipulated his characters to suit his own ends. So however satisfactory *Brideshead* remains to Catholics and Catholic fellow travelers, it is a flawed and in some cases infuriating performance for those who do not share Waugh's faith.

Waugh fretted over *Brideshead*. I have mentioned the revisions; his preface to what I suppose should be called the "authorized" edition is apologetic in tone and asks, if not the indulgence, at least the sympathetic cooperation of the reader in judging scenes and speeches such as Julia's peroration on mortal sin. But in his diary Waugh referred to *Brideshead* as "the first of my novels," by which he meant that his theme henceforth was to be Catholicism and that his books pursuing this theme would be the most significant of his career. Accordingly he set to work on *Helena* (1950) on May 6, 1945; progress on the manuscript was slow, and one suspects that he was all too ready to be diverted by the success of *Brideshead*, which was published May 28. Other diversions followed: trips to Germany, Spain, and the United States; editorial, journalistic, and literary projects including *Scott King's Modern Europe* (1947) and *The Loved One*. Although he steadfastly maintained otherwise, Waugh must have realized in the more honest recesses of his mind that *Helena* was a bad book; this, more than the press of affairs, probably accounts for the fact that he took five years to complete the novel.

Here, more than in any other of his Catholic narratives, Waugh's material works against him. Recent advances in ecumenism notwithstanding, nothing is as likely to engender the scorn of Protestant and freethinker alike as the Catholic veneration of relics. And no relics are more holy or more notorious, depending on one's orientation, than fragments of the cross on which Christ was crucified. Waugh knew this. In the preface to *Helena* he defended his novel by refuting the ancient canard that, taken together, the pieces of the true cross at large in the world add up to more wood than the cross contained in the first place. But there was still the problem of whether the location of the cross was disclosed to Helena in a dream. Most Catholic authorities think it was not. Waugh doubtless also knew this, as well as the fact that contemporary scholarly opinion holds that Helena was the daughter of a tavern keeper and not, as the old myth and Waugh would have it, a princess, the offspring of King Coel.

These are relatively minor matters. Of greater importance is the unsuitability of Waugh's fictional method to any kind of historical material. In the *Paris Review* interview Waugh told Julian Jebb that Jebb was raising the wrong questions by asking him to talk about characterization in the ordinary fictional sense. What he did, Waugh declared, he did with language—which seems certainly to be true. Far more than most writers, he used the tonal qualities of words and sentences and an exaggerated accuracy of dialogue to delineate character and to define theme. His revisions again and again involved exchanges of conversation between people. The success of his fiction depended greatly on what the characters said. Waugh's language and that of his characters lifted his work into realms both satirical and transcendent, but always he began with truth, with startling fidelity of phrasing and vocabulary, whether his scene was a party in Mayfair or the court in Azania or an embalming room in California. But how did Romans talk around the forum and out in the hinterlands during the early part of the fourth century? Waugh could not know, and this ignorance, which proved to be only an inconvenience to such writers as Robert Graves and Marguerite Yourcenar, rendered Waugh literally all but impotent. In *Helena* one looks in vain for conversations such as Charles and Cara have in *Brideshead*, in which Lord Marchmain's motives and the relationship between Charles and Sebastian are adumbrated. Never does the prose in *Helena* achieve the high level of energy found in most of Waugh's other works. His material and the meaning he seeks in it seem always to elude him. This may be partly because of the magnitude of his theme, but certainly the failure of his language is the major cause. Except for isolated passages the prose is flat, and the novel is finally unsuccessful.

Waugh's crowning achievement is *Sword of Honor* (1965). Even more than was the case with *Brideshead*, its last revisions were made in public. Waugh originally planned a novel, perhaps two, based on his experiences in the war. He wrote and published a trilogy, then cut and rewrote and combined the three volumes into one. Here Waugh finds his old voice, but with a difference. Gone is the baroque ornamentation that for many critics marred the texture of *Brideshead*. The strategies used in his earlier work to defend against the chaos and the pain of life—ironic detachment, romanticism, humor, and nostalgia—are subordinated and through much of the novel entirely effaced. With strength drawn from religious faith and the example of his saintly father, Guy Crouchback embraces human experience as none of Waugh's other characters does.

A commonly voiced criticism of *Brideshead* is that in the book Waugh equated the Catholic church and the English aristocracy. The charge is exaggerated, given the disintegration of the Flyte family; but the tensions of the novel, the conflicts between mundane and transcendent values, are developed within the boundaries of Marchmain grandeur. In *Sword* the enveloping action consists of the army, the bureaucracy, and the civilian world. If the emphasis remains upper class—officers, assistant ministers, and members of Bellamy's—there are soldiers and refugees enough to fill out the image and make it representative of the world at large. In *Brideshead* the house, stripped and defaced by the military authorities who use it as a headquarters, represents the decline of social order and another step in the destruction of old monuments that had begun with the dismantling of March-main House. In *Sword of Honor* the Sword of Stalingrad, on display at Westminster Abbey, symbolizes the abandonment by Western civilization of the religious and political princi-ples on which it was based and according to which it has, until now, survived.

In *Brideshead* Lady Marchmain's Catholicism is rigid and at times rebarbative, and Lord Marchmain's last-minute re-pentance is for many readers ill prepared. No such charges can be leveled against *Sword of Honor*. Gervase Crouch-back's faith is humane and gentle, and even Uncle Peregrine, who can hardly force himself to think of converts as real Catholics, is a comic figure who helps bring Virginia into the Church. And Peregrine is only one aspect of Waugh's prepara-tion for Virginia's conversion. She is married and divorced from Guy before the novel opens, and her pregnancy by Trim-mer sends her back to Guy.

At the end of *Brideshead* Charles Ryder has like Virginia become a Catholic; but unlike Guy Crouchback he has not come to understand his own humanity in terms of his faith. Guy progresses from a state of spiritual malaise—accidie, as some of Waugh's critics have properly designated it—to an understanding of his culpability, a perception of the faults inherent in his pursuit of goals that are undeniably good. Ryder takes comfort in visiting the chapel at Brideshead and in reciting newly learned prayers. By remarrying Virginia and after her death by raising Trimmer's son, Guy makes repara-tion, which is never totally a personal matter. Reparation for one's own sins involves the penitent in a common reparation for the sins of the world.

Perhaps we should study Waugh's work by starting with the end and working back toward the beginning: begin with *Sword of Honor*, an extraordinary accomplishment, and try to understand his earlier fiction as a long preparation for his final achievement. By doing so, we might see Waugh himself in a different light. In some respects his last years were a paradigm of human weakness. The hallucinations that were the basis for *The Ordeal of Gilbert Pinfold* (1957) resulted from Waugh's ingestion of too many drugs and too much liquor. He regained his mental equilibrium, but he spent most of his time brooding in his study, going to parties, and occasionally giving rein to his notoriously bad disposition. He was not writing: between Easter, 1965, and his death at Easter, 1966, there are not even any entries in his diary. From a literary standpoint, his final months were a total waste. But there was an element of submission in them too, and in his weakness he may, like Guy Crouchback, have found the kind of strength that he had sought and finally discovered in his novels.

The Two Worlds of William Golding

If, as Yeats claimed, a source of literature is the author's argument with himself, then William Golding's success as a novelist is easy to account for. When he was young, as he has said many times, he was a political liberal who believed that the human condition could be ameliorated by social action. Redistribute the wealth and abolish poverty; end poverty and eradicate crime; the fault was not in us, but in the system. Then came World War II, and Golding underwent not so much a change of heart as of understanding. It was not that people were killing each other, he said. As a classicist he knew this had been going on for millennia. But the crimes of Hitler and Stalin were, he thought, peculiar to our unhappy century; beyond that, and perhaps most important, he discovered during his service in the navy that his fellow countrymen were innately evil. Forced to live close to each other aboard ship, they lost their civilized veneer of manners and morals and grew petty and selfish and sometimes vicious. Finally, Golding concluded that most people of whatever nationality were potential Nazis; England and America had escaped such a fate because of accidental turns in the historical process.

Such was the genesis of *Lord of the Flies* (1954), Golding's first novel, which is the story of a group of boys placed on an Edenic island beyond the influence of organized society. Here they reprise the fall of man and the evil that follows. "Fancy thinking the Beast was something you could hunt and kill," the Lord of the Flies says to Simon, the mystic. "You knew, didn't you? I'm a part of you? . . . I'm the reason why it's no go?" The boys make rules by which they hope to govern themselves, but their dark natures turn some of them into sadists and murderers. They kill first Simon and then Piggy, who represents the rational aspect of human nature, and are trying to kill Ralph, the hero of the narrative, when help arrives. That the book made Golding's point was evidenced by the mail he received congratulating him on telling the truth about people. But as he thought about the novel later, Golding was not entirely comfortable with what he had done. He continued to believe in original sin. But he believed too that the best way to deal with it was by a socialistic system, which with modifications was what he had believed before he wrote *Lord of the Flies.*

Golding's divided psyche is also present in the mystical force pervading much of his other work. *Pincher Martin* (1956), the story of a naval officer who dies in the war, is a direct and orthodox treatment of Christian eschatology. Christopher Martin is called "Pincher" because he pinches everything: the wives and sweethearts of his friends; the best parts of plays; notice from the powerful; fame; money. He compares himself to the last slug in a Chinese box, the one that has eaten all the others and grown fat. The story is a *tour de force.* What appears to be an account of Martin's effort to survive on a rock in the ocean after his ship has been torpedoed is discovered at the end of the book to be his judgment, his ultimate rejection of God's grace. The theology could not be more conventional. Martin is possessed by pride and gluttony. His determination to survive on his rock is the chronicle of his refusal to submit his ego to the will of God. He has damned himself by the life he has lived, the persona his vices have created that cannot be changed in the moment of his dying.

Free Fall (1959) is about free will and the loss thereof and the contending forces of empirical science and religious mystery. At the beginning of the story, Sammy Mountjoy is exploring his past, searching for the point at which he lost his freedom—a quest that raises some familiar existential questions. Who is he, and where is he, and how can he reconcile intention and act and the fragments of reality as he perceives them? He becomes in turn a student, the betrayer of an innocent girl, a famous artist, a prisoner of war. In this novel Golding wrote of the opposite of his own experience. He is a writer, so he made his hero a painter; he was raised in middle-class comfort, so he plunged the youthful Mountjoy into poverty; he had been a sailor, so he put Sammy into the army.

Free Fall is a brilliantly written novel, and in one of its aspects it develops an unexceptional Christian treatment of means and ends. Sammy pursues and seduces Beatrice, uses and then abandons her. At the end of the story he visits her in a sanitarium where, mentally deranged, she urinates on his shoes. Has he destroyed her? Would she still have gone insane if he had not left her? These are questions he can never answer, but they relate only to the degree of his guilt. He has learned that you can have anything you want if you are willing to pay the price for it, but the price is usually too high. The means, which seem to be justified by the ends they seek, infect the ends with their own corruption. So it is with Sammy's possession of Beatrice, but his turpitude reflects the moral uncertainty of a divided world.

The universe operates according to natural laws. The stars maintain their orbits. Penicillin cures pneumonia. The atom splits on demand. Scientists assert the reality of the natural world they have codified, leaving no space for mystery and God. But science begs the fundamental questions that seek to learn the purpose of creation. These are answered by the mystic, whose realm of faith and revelation postulates a system of reality that neither microscope nor equation can discern. Both the world of science and that of theology exist. Both claim to tell the truth, and each claim is valid. Our tragedy is that the two realms are inimical to each other, and they make

separate demands on our minds and hearts. We lose our freedom and commit ourselves to mistaken action in the reflection of this division within ourselves.

Was life simpler before science challenged the hegemony
of faith? Probably it was, but a Christian ambience imposes
its own kind of complexity. To live in Salisbury, as Golding
does, is to spend your days in the presence of an architectural
myth. In 1220 Bishop Richard Poore, weary of bickering between his priests and the soldiers stationed at Old Sarum, laid
the cornerstone for a new cathedral on the swampy land of
Salisbury Plain. The building proceeded without interrup-
tion; the cloisters and chapter house were added before the
turn of the century. Then in 1330 the bishop or, as Golding
has it in his novel, the dean decided that the cathedral needed
a spire. There is no information on how the spire was constructed. All that is really known is that it is too heavy for the
walls of the cathedral to support. The columns at the tran-
septs bend under its weight. Four hundred feet high, it sways
in the wind and is almost constantly under repair, but it endures. In clear weather it can be seen from a great dis-
tance. Whether in fog or sunlight it dominates the city and the
country around it, and it nagged at Golding's imagination
until he wrote *The Spire* (1964).

Jocelin conceives of his planned spire as a "prayer in
stone," but other members of the cathedral chapter view it
less generously. At the beginning of the novel, construction
has begun, the building is filled with dust, and ecclesiastical
routine has been disrupted. Masses must be said in the Lady
Chapel. The main altar is in disarray; side altars and chantries
are forced into desuetude. At first priestly complaints against
this temporary inconvenience seem petty, but they become
more serious when Roger Mason, the master builder, predicts
disaster, and walls and columns creak and bow under the
increasing weight. Jocelin's "prayer in stone" becomes his
obsession. In the firm conviction that he is doing God's work,

he abandons mass and matins, ceases to confess or pray, and devotes all his time and energy to construction. To keep Roger Mason on the job, he cajoles, then threatens, and finally collaborates in Mason's seduction of Goody Pangall, wife of a sexton, which results in her death as she attempts to bear Mason's child.

Golding's knowledge of medieval society endows *The Spire* with a strong sense of time and place—the clothes people wore, the food they ate, the routines they followed. Overlaying this is his inescapably modern point of view. In the opening chapter, a model of the cathedral is seen to resemble a recumbent man with the spire as phallus. Jocelin is in love with Goody Pangall, and his desire for her helps shape his determination to build the spire and further complicates his complicity in her seduction by Roger. As we come to learn, Jocelin's position as dean was secured for him by his aunt while she was mistress to the king. This knowledge engenders Jocelin's awakening to himself. He had thought he was doing the work of God. But there is no innocent work, he decides, and only God can be sure what God's true work is.

The imagery in this novel is stunning. At the end, a broken Jocelin escapes from what will soon be his deathbed to visit and seek the forgiveness of an idle and besotted Roger Mason. Near the wall of the cathedral close, he sees what he takes momentarily to be angels, but soon recognizes as apple blossoms bright in sunlight, shaken by wind. He finds the tree with its complex symbolism a cause for weeping. The fruit that the tree soon will bear suggests the Garden of Eden and man's fall; the blossoms speak of spring and rejuvenation. An instant later he sees the flash of a kingfisher's wing. "Come back," he says. Then in his newfound humility he reprimands himself for asking, believing himself unworthy of the salvation that this ancient symbol of Christ promises. The ambiguity of his situation is not resolved: the saving host is placed on his tongue after he has died, imperfectly shriven. The spire, which cost several lives and perhaps some souls as well, continues to stand, fulfillment of Jocelin's prayer and monument to his ego.

Darkness Visible (1979), Golding's most recent exploration of the mystical, is a grim work indeed. Septimus Windrave or Windrove or Windgrave—our uncertainty about his name symbolizes the elusive nature of his character—appears like some wingless phoenix out of the fires of the London blitz. The disfigurement of his scars sets him apart; his efforts at friendship are commonly rebuffed. He is offered affection only by Mr. Pedigree, a teacher at the Foundlings School, who is homosexual. When Mr. Pedigree is discharged from his job, Septimus attempts to assuage the guilt he feels by fasting and memorizing Scripture. He is visited by creatures from another realm—one is blue, the other is red—who bring with them the intense cold that accompanies all demonic apparitions. Yet they speak of salvation and expiation, and they are as difficult to categorize as is Septimus.

Impinging on Septimus' life, but never a part of it, are the careers of twin girls, exquisitely beautiful and utterly delinquent children. Mistreated by their father, who imposes a succession of mistresses on the household, they would be prime material for a sociologist's casebook except that they are not simply bad: they are evil. One of them becomes a prostitute, not for money but out of a desire to do the wrong thing; she soon discovers that her soul requires a more essential depravity. She turns to kidnapping and general viciousness, and her sister becomes a political terrorist. Septimus sees these girls and knows them, but can never become close to them any more than he can establish affectionate contact with the honest citizens whose paths cross his. He is different from everyone else not only because of his scars, but also because of his gift for prophecy, his insight into the unseen world as well as an acquaintance with those who populate it. What Golding seems to establish in this book is the fact that the supernatural operates within quotidian life, but neither he nor we nor Septimus is supposed to see it in all its dimensions or to understand its operations. Knowledge of its existence enhances our perception of mundane reality and sharpens our moral vision.

Darkness Visible is better written and more richly evocative than *Lord of the Flies*, but it is neither more nor less pessimistic. In both books, as in all the other novels mentioned here, the rational part of Golding's psyche is engaged with his religious impulse, which manifests itself not in liturgical practice or theological investigations, but in his keen sense of another reality wherein evil breeds alongside good and helps to endow our natures. But as with most writers, Golding's dark vision is lightened by time. When it appeared, *Darkness Visible* was the first novel Golding had published in twelve years. It was followed immediately by *Rites of Passage* (1980), which contains no demons or angels but in which a clergyman's fall from grace is a key sequence in the narrative. The time is the early nineteenth century. Edmund Talbot, on his way to Australia in a dilapidated warship given over to passenger service, keeps a journal for his influential godfather, who is sponsoring him in what Edmund hopes will be a distinguished diplomatic career. The journal and a letter written by an Anglican priest named Colley comprise the text of the book.

Edmund is vain, judgmental, and self-centered, but he has good manners and wit, and there is charm in his seeming to be perfectly typical of his time in history and his station in life. The ship on which he is sailing is too small to accommodate a full complement of fools, but Golding offers us a fair sampling of human types. There are Brocklebank, a painter, who claims to be traveling with his wife and daughter but who is actually maintaining a *ménage à trois*; Prettiman, a political activist, who is taking a printing press with him to Australia and who parades the deck with a blunderbuss hoping to kill an albatross and slay superstition with a single shot; Miss Granham, a governess somewhat embittered by her social station; *la famille* Pike, as Edmund calls them, man and wife and two daughters; Bowles, who "has something to do" with the law; the Reverend Colley; the stern captain of the ship; a full roster of sailors and midshipmen; and a largely nameless group of second-class passengers.

During the first two-thirds of the story some tension is developed by the weather, which tosses and then becalms the ship, and by the passengers' fear that they might be attacked by the French, with whom the English are at war. But most of the drama evolves out of disparities of view and temperament among the passengers and between them and Captain Anderson, whose quarterdeck is off limits to all but the crew who are standing watch. Talbot pronounces the name of his noble godfather and thereby secures special privileges. Other passengers are content to take the air where they are told, but the Reverend Colley, pursuing what he thinks is his pastoral duty, pesters Captain Anderson and is badly used by both officers and men.

Golding's style has never been better than it is here. His use of sharp detail and skillful dialogue brings even his most minor characters to life. The frequent rocking of the ship, which makes most of the passengers sick, enhances our sense of their frail humanity. They dose themselves with the purser's paregoric—sold at increasingly higher prices as the voyage lengthens—form and reform liaisons, and reshape their opinions of each other. Talbot's point of view, superior but tolerant, unifies the narrative, though at its most crucial point the story is taken over by Colley. This is a bold bit of construction that Golding is able to bring off. Colley has gone to the forecastle intending to conduct services for the crew and the second-class passengers. Instead he joins the revels in progress, gets drunk, returns to his cabin, takes to his bed, and dies. Why he should succumb to shame cannot be convincingly answered by a simple disclosure of the overt act, nor can the character development necessary to convince us that Colley would die of shame be conveyed through Talbot's journal.

Golding introduces a long letter from Colley to his sister, in which much of the material that has been covered in Talbot's journal is recapitulated from Colley's point of view. Finally we learn that he has done something he did not think himself capable of. Not being able to forgive himself or to foresee his own redemption, he dies.

This is a sad story, and Golding does not make light of it. Yet the death of Colley cannot fully counteract the sense of joy Golding takes in his characters and his plot. The end of the novel finds the ship still at sea. Two of its people are missing—Colley and a servant of the first-class passengers who has fallen overboard—and a pregnant woman traveling in the bow of the ship has had a miscarriage. But life goes on, and in spite of storm and adversity there is happiness as well as sorrow. The novel is *comédie humaine* on a high level, and after a seven-year interval Golding evidently decided that the material was too good to abandon. There is no indication at the end of *Rites of Passage* that another volume is to come, and Golding's next novel was *Paper Men* (1984), a well-written but slight tale of the relationship between a writer and a literary scholar. *Close Quarters* (1987) continues Talbot's narrative and announces Golding's intention to make the work into a trilogy.

Early in *Close Quarters* Edmund and his companions, their ship becalmed once more on a foggy sea, find themselves drifting toward a larger vessel that they take to be a French man-of-war. They declare their intention to be heroic and make their feckless preparations to fight, but the other ship is English and brings news that the war with France is over. Better still, Sir Henry Somerset, captain of the *Alcyone*, has with him his wife and her ward, Marion Chumley, whose first appearance is for Edmund a *coup de foudre*. Lightning strikes, and in an instant Miss Chumley is his heart's desire. Marion is penniless, dependent on the beneficence of Lady Somerset, and therefore unable to help the career of the ambitious and, to this point, calculating Edmund. But he is smitten, and nothing else matters. His behavior is a parody of the tradition of romantic love in English literature. He mopes, he cannot sleep, he quotes poetry and speaks foolishness. Marion is responsive, but as befits a lady her compliments are less extravagant than his. The lovers are at once comic and attractive. We laugh at them and envy their innocence; we wish them well and recognize in them the capacity for affection that helps sustain our lives. Because the ships will have to part when the wind rises, Edmund presses Miss Chumley to continue her voyage with Captain Anderson. He moves into the cabin lately occupied by Colley, so that Marion may have his, but such an arrangement is not countenanced by Lady Somerset; the lovers are forced to part.

This is fortunate for Marion. In a moment of carelessness by an officer, the masts of Edmund's ship are broken, further disabling a vessel that is afflicted by age and whose progress is impeded by seaweed growing on her bottom. The vegetation must be removed from the hull or the ship will never make port, but whether the rotting hull can endure a scraping is doubtful. After the interval of love we have the threat of death, which, as Golding presents it here, is both bitter and comic. Wheeler, the servant who fell overboard in *Rites of Passage*, reappears in *Close Quarters*, having been rescued by Sir Henry's *Alcyone*. Memories of his near death by water make the idea of drowning unbearable to him; he shoots himself rather than risk sinking.

The purser is less fearful. He has posted a thousand-pound reward for his own rescue and depends on human greed, of which he is the avatar, to effect his physical salvation. The sailors, eager for recompense, will save him first, he thinks, and he has provisioned a lifeboat for that purpose. In the meantime he presses his debtors to pay what they owe, a good deal of humor being engendered by their refusal. Edmund declines to pay for the paregoric he has consumed, saying he bought it from the now-deceased Wheeler. But he does pay for a watertight cask in which he will save his journal. Inviting others to share the cask, he collects from most of the passengers and crew "some small package, some object, a ring, a bauble, a book—a journal!—something, anything which, whatever it was, would seem by its survival to prolong a vestige of life." Everyone prepares for death. Quarrels are made up. Friendships become closer. Enmities that remain are deepened. One of the Pike children is seriously ill, depleted by constant seasickness. Edmund believes she should be put in a hammock, a remedy Lord Nelson devised against the same malady. But no one listens to him, and so death actual—as in Wheeler's case—and potential haunts the close of the second volume.

Fire Down Below (1989) continues the story, as Edmund's increasingly enfeebled ship makes its passage toward what the passengers and crew hope will be Australia. Their navigation is uncertain. Much of the time they are moving through fog, and some of the instruments are out of kilter. The competition between Edmund's friend Lieutenant Summers and Summers' rival Lieutenant Benét is exacerbated by their disagreement over how their course should be charted and how a new mainmast might be raised. Benét's plan, which is executed, is to fix the mast to its wooden base with hot metal rods, which will tighten in the wood as they cool. Summers fears that the heated iron will start a fire, and it does, but the ship does not burst into flame until it has reached Australia. Not everyone survives the voyage. The purser and the indefatigably optimistic midshipman Taylor perish in an unnecessary effort to save themselves when the ship achieves a near miss with an iceberg. Scant sadness accrues here. Jones will be mourned by neither passengers nor crew, and Taylor, who saw all life as a joke, must have taken the same view of death and met his fate giggling.

All this and other accidents of the voyage and the happy ending that follows are developed with great skill. One of Golding's major strengths is his ability to master the language and manners and physical details of other times and places. His command of nautical terms and his knowledge of old ships and how they worked are even more impressive than his creation of the world of medieval clerics in *The Spire*. But the character and personality of Edmund give the story its life and make all of Golding's literary devices succeed. From the beginning of the trilogy Edmund engages our sympathy, but months at sea change him from a supercilious young man, self-centered and judgmental, to a more mature actor in and observer of the human scene. Miss Granham, the discontented governess, marries Mr. Prettiman, the liberal reformer. Edmund, though still pining for Miss Chumley, last seen in *Close Quarters* sailing away on the *Alcyone*, feels a strong attraction for Mrs. Prettiman and is enticed into considering her and her husband's political ideas. Edmund abandons neither his principles nor his upbringing, but his sympathy for other people and their notions of morality is enhanced.

Edmund's mental seduction by Mrs. Prettiman—their relationship never even borders on the physical except in Edmund's mind—is both important in itself and a means of bringing into focus the modifications that experience has worked in Edmund's character. Forced to live week after week in near proximity to people of all stations and attitudes and degrees of probity, he is obligated to regard the complex conditions of men and be affected by what he observes. Except that women are added in the narrative, Edmund's experience is not much different than Golding's must have been when he served with the Royal Navy and returned to write his first novel with its theme of original sin. Compared with *Lord of the Flies*, the trilogy is a gentle and hopeful document. The outrageous and wholly satisfactory ending, at which Golding himself pokes fun, sends Edmund back to England with Miss Chumley at his side, his family enriched by the death of his godfather and he made a member of Parliament by the same stroke of luck. In the final chapter he addresses us long after

the fact of his voyage. He has mellowed greatly. But he still
appeals to us as essentially the same well-meaning but snob-
bish young man who boarded the dilapidated English man-o'-
war on the first page of *Rites of Passage*.

Part of the art here is in Golding's mature vision of a world
that is evil and often cruel and always uncertain. Every bad
thing that he has depicted in his previous novels remains
true. But there is joy too, of living and of surviving, and there
is even some comfort in remembering those, like Edmund's
friend Lieutenant Summers, who do not survive. Summers
has clearly been bested in his rivalry with Benét, who has
become Captain Anderson's favorite and whose rapid ad-
vancement is a given among the Australian bureaucrats.
Summers is made captain of the unseaworthy ship on which
he served and Edmund traveled. It will spend the rest of its
few days in the harbor. The fire, started when Benét's plan to
raise the mainmast was followed, flames up; the ship ex-
plodes, and Summers dies. But he had at the last his command and his captain's epaulette. Golding's tone here is
superb—ironic, charitable, optimistic, and, most of all, light-
hearted in the face of the grim turns that life frequently takes.
We should trust the tone and the narrative itself and not look
for profundities, Golding seems to tell his readers in dialogue
spoken by Mrs. Prettiman to Edmund: "The voyage has been
a considerable part of your whole life, sir. Do not refine upon
its nature. As I told you, it was not an Odyssey. It is not type,
emblem, metaphor of the human condition. It is, or rather it
was, what it was. A series of events."

This is at once good advice and less than the truth. Because
of the brilliance of Golding's writing, the fruit of his mature
way of viewing the life that he has shown us before in other
manifestations and dimensions, this narrative, devoid as it
may be of symbols, nonetheless generates its own happy profundity. It is Golding's version of *The Tempest*. The two
worlds of good and evil, of the spiritual and the mundane,

persist and defy reconciliation with each other. Mischief continues as a major element in human endeavor. Life is largely composed of the follies of those who live it. But Edmund's good heart encompasses all and celebrates all and makes all endurable. Such is the nature of Golding's mature vision.

Part III

In Praise of Blood Sports

It is a disproportionate business, the killing of animals. Now and then a boat capsizes and duck hunters drown or freeze to death before they can build a fire or find shelter. Quail hunters shoot themselves climbing fences. Deer hunters shoot each other, and recently a dentist in my part of the world fell from his deer stand in a tree and was fatally injured. But by and large it is the animals that die: however much hunters may complain about the lack of game and the receding wilderness and the belligerence of farmers, the odds favor the man. Even a mediocre marksman who has found the right spot in a dove field will make his limit in an hour, and if no warden is nearby, he is likely to shoot two or three times as much as the law allots him. This is because people are smarter than birds and more perfidious. The dove wants to eat, the man wants to kill, but the two desires are hardly in balance. The hunter knows that he need merely hide behind his bale of hay or stand still in the shadow of his tree, and the dove, unable to learn from experience or unwilling to do what experience dictates, returns to be shot at again and even again, if he survives to do so. On the best days, from the hunter's point of view, birds fly continually and fall continually, fluttering down on wings that will no longer support them or dropping still and straight to the ground. There is no end to this as long as there is game. I once read of a nineteenth-century English gentleman who bagged 250,000 birds in the course of an ordinary lifespan. Killing does not diminish the urge to kill. Blood lust thrives on its own fulfillment. If today is a good day, we must go again tomorrow because then the shooting may be even better.

I know all this from observation, but the authorization for blood sports is in Genesis. God made the animals, pronouncing them good, and then made man, giving him dominion over them. How this arrangement may have worked had Satan not intervened we can only speculate. There might never have been guns in Eden, or weapons of any kind. Adam and Eve and their descendants might have been vegetarians, but one thing is certain: there would have been no need for the mediation of rituals. As Robert Penn Warren has remarked, "There will be no literature in Heaven." A race perfected and delivered from death will require no parables or images or correlatives. No accommodation need be struck with immortality, and in Paradise we will know things for what they essentially are. We will have the sort of angelic intelligence that Allen Tate castigated us for trying to exercise before we possessed it. But between the fall and the final judgment, we live with our limited powers of perception and with a knowledge of death that must be propitiated. This is what hunting at its best is about. This is the theme of the literature of hunting.

In "The Last Day in the Field," Caroline Gordon's Aleck Maury sits on his back porch in the early days of autumn, playing with his fishing tackle and telling himself that he will not hunt this year because of an arthritic leg that will not endure the walking. He is an old man, conscious as old men are of his own mortal frailty. Here at the beginning of her story, Gordon uses an image at once felicitous and familiar. The elderberry bushes by the stable are already yellow near the ground. Their green tops wait for a heavy frost that Maury knows is coming. "Ah-ha, it'll get you yet," he says, picking up the old metaphor of autumn and death on which Gordon will ring changes for the rest of the narrative. That night the big frost descends, stripping the leaves from a hickory tree, and the next morning Maury sets out with a young friend to hunt, bad leg notwithstanding.

Joe Thompson, Maury's companion, is twenty and deficient both in skill and wisdom. Maury can school him in the techniques of the field, as years ago older men taught him. He tells Joe when and how to shoot, admonishing him not to try to outthink the dogs, but knowledge derived from ritual is perfected in memory. Initiation begins with the stories that the old people tell by which the young measure their own experience. The education of Faulkner's Ike McCaslin starts with conversation. The tales that Sam Fathers tells of his own ancestors put Ike's first killing of a deer into the context of an unwritten history. What stories Joe Thompson might have heard we do not know, but he is linked to the past by the dogs he brings to the hunt and by his friendship with Maury. The dogs are the last ever trained by Charley Morrison, a friend of Maury's who shot himself, perhaps deliberately, when he found himself, like Maury, getting too old to hunt.

For Maury the hunting ritual has reached a point of equilibrium. His eye for terrain is similar to that of an accomplished general. He knows where the birds are likely to be found, and he knows how to put himself in the right position when they break their cover. He is an expert at the business of shooting quail; as his skill has developed, so has his consciousness of his own mortality, until both have now reached their ultimate fruition. His own doom is symbolically and actually consonant with the last bird he will kill, a single that soars high above a tree to be silhouetted in the setting sun before Maury drops him. This is how the story ends: with Maury knowing that he will never again do one of the things that he has loved most to do. He knows that his life is significantly reduced. He is deprived in a way that mimics the final, total deprivation. Bitter as this moment is for Maury, it is one of fulfillment too; it is the inevitable end for which he has been rehearsing. In every death he has caused, he has been a participant.

Andrew Lytle's "The Mahogany Frame" is also about death, but death perceived in terms of a different kind of initiation. The main character is a well-mannered, properly raised southern boy, and Lytle emphasizes his youth by never revealing his name; he is referred to as the "boy" or "kid" throughout the story. His innocence is extraordinary even by the standards of 1945, when the story was initially published. Receiving his first pair of long trousers, he senses that he has symbolically put on the clothes of manhood, but when his older brother admonishes him to "keep his pants buttoned," he fails to get the joke. His understanding has been formed by his mother, who has taught him the rules of honorable be-havior largely by keeping before him the example of his dead great-grandfather, whose portrait hangs near the mantel in a mahogany frame. According to the mother, Grandfather Laus—short for Menelaus—was the avatar of all proper con-duct and generous instincts. He stood erect, looked everyone in the eye, kept his promises, treated women with gentle solicitude, and told nothing but the truth. This romantic fig-ure is fleshed out with anecdote: He almost fought a duel with Andrew Jackson because of a horse race; during hunting season he slept on the ground, bagged game of every sort, and once brought home a live bear. A devoted family man, he traced patterns of quilts to take home for his wife to copy, and he received the "mantle of grace" at the Methodist church. That such a paragon might be too good to be true has never crossed the boy's mind. When the boy's Uncle Bomar sug-gests that Laus was a "rounder," the boy defends his great-grandfather, and for the time being Bomar lets the matter drop.

Still, entering the ambience of duck hunters is itself a kind of initiation for which the boy is unprepared. He and Bomar are to shoot at the same lake where Laus once hunted, but surely in Laus's time men did not call each other "bastard" and "son of a bitch" even in jest or make loose talk with waitresses at the hunting lodge. To the boy, everything is alien. His body is shaken by the cold of the lake, and he is embarrassed by questions he asks that expose his ignorance. He does not see the first duck to come in range until the guide has killed it. As the day wears on, the boy learns from the guide Goosetree how to wait and to watch and to shoot at the right time, even though he usually misses. In teaching the boy the rudiments of hunting, and at the same time denigrating the trade that he follows, the guide—which is the title Lytle first gave to the story—prepares the boy for his true passage into manhood.

The boy thinks that being a guide, hunting every day in season and getting paid for it, would be a nearly perfect occupation; but when he asks Goosetree if his son will "follow in your footsteps," the guide replies: "Hell, no. There's no money in guiding." The boy suggests that the adventure of the job might make it attractive, but Goosetree insists that guiding "gets stale." He has bought a hunting lodge that he intends to rent out. Often, he tells the boy, men come to the lake with women, and most of the time the women are not their wives. Consummate hunter though he is, Goosetree would prefer to live on his rents, no questions asked of the renter. For the boy this is a shocking preamble for what his uncle will say about his great-grandfather.

Late in the morning Bomar and his guide, who have been hunting in another part of the lake, join the boy and Goosetree. They have been working their way through a bottle of whisky, and when the boy sees coots and mistakes them for ducks, Bomar asks ironically what the distinguished Laus would think of a great-grandson who could not tell mallards from mudhens. Ostensibly speaking to his own guide, his voice fraught with irony, he offers his own version of the character of Laus. The old man, according to Bomar, had done everything he wanted to do and had gotten away with it. He had managed to play the horses and chase women without damaging his reputation for probity or disturbing his own domestic tranquillity. He had kept his wife busy raising children and making quilts until he got too old to roam; then he settled down to the exemplary life and the business of adding luster to his own reputation. After his death his fame continued to grow because, as Bomar has told the boy earlier, women "like 'em dead." Once buried, they can be remade along virtuous lines and they cause no trouble. "Don't take it too hard, kid," Bomar says. "You aren't the first one to take a wooden nickel."

The boy is confused; even the idiom Bomar has employed is beyond his comprehension. For him, revelation will not come simply with words, though through the empty afternoon Bomar's text is glossed by the guides, who speak of sex and infidelity. Then suddenly the ducks return, and for the boy knowledge is rendered complete by ritual. He rises in the boat, makes a clean kill, and knows for the first time the hunter's moment of realization: the feeling of detachment and integration, of his own isolation in the world and his communion with it and with the life he has just destroyed. The hunters congratulate each other, and more ducks come. Bomar and the boy, shooting simultaneously at the same duck, make the kill together. Caught up in this shared moment of the ritual of death, the boy and Bomar turn to each other, and what Bomar has said about the boy's great-grandfather is confirmed by a similarity between Bomar and Laus that the boy has never before noticed. The eyes that he now looks into are identical with those that stare from the face in the mahogany frame.

Lytle's story is more complicated and less romantic than "The Last Day in the Field." Charley Morrison, who trained dogs and shot quail and probably killed himself when he got too old to hunt, is left by Gordon to rest in peace, his faults buried with him. Aleck Maury is married, we know, but that is all we are told about him. Whether he is a faithful husband, a devoted father, a lover of horseflesh, a good provider are not aspects of her story. We can assume that at some point in his life Maury has gone through the same initiation as "the boy," but now he is old and that experience is far behind him.

Every year that we live brings us closer to death, and as the years pass, our minds focus more sharply on mortality. We may be irascible, proud, envious, rebellious, all of which are faults, but deterioration of the flesh delivers us from our more flamboyant transgressions. As Augustine said, we outgrow our carnal sins. Maury's killing of his last bird is a ritual almost as pure in its intent as a funeral service. He is appeasing death and, in a small way, transcending it. He causes it, participates in it, and deprives it of some of its terror by seeing it up close. More than this, Maury understands the necessity for death, the natural and metaphysical propriety of it. Dying may be an end or, as Stonewall Jackson called it at the hour of his own death, a translation. It may be finality or a beginning; in either case it is logical, and in either case the logic inheres in the ritual. However often it is repeated, the ritual continues to inform. Gordon renders all this in action and in image—a fine achievement.

In Lytle's story—and this is typical of Lytle's fiction and his criticism—the boy is introduced to death in the same way that Adam and Eve were: by acquiring the knowledge of good and evil. For them, sex became sex as we think of it only after the fall. They looked at each other and knew they were naked, and the fig leaves gave them away. Seeing their shame, God expelled them from the Garden; deprived of Paradise, they entered into what we have since come to call the human condition. They became mortal and knew it; but the knowledge of death followed the other knowledge that perverted their understanding of sensuality. So it is with the boy. Not only is the killing of the ducks meaningless to him until Bomar has told him the truth about his great-grandfather; his skill at shooting and the feeling that accompanies it are delayed until his innocence is vitiated. This is the old literary business of linking sex and death made new by Lytle's sophisticated use of the hunting ritual. A clever critic might discover many symbols in this story: the chill in the air; the lake; the boat hidden in the rushes; the progress of the day; and the sudden abundance of game when the time for shooting is over. But everything depends from the ritual of death and of knowledge.

Always in hunting stories—certainly in those of Faulkner, even in those of Hemingway in which the existential hero must search continually for some way to deal with his own mortality—the thrust is outward. The fictional hunter is, in his small or not so small way, the Nietzschean tragic figure, the synthesis of the Apollonian and Dionysian impulses. At his best, he lives in an equilibrium between his consciousness of himself as a unique individual and the knowledge that he is a part of universal nature, to which ultimately his individual self will have to submit. An aspect of his struggle is to continue to see his own separate existence as a part of and as dependent on something much larger and vastly more important than himself. Faulkner makes this particularly clear in "The Bear." To find his own identity, to have what he most wants, Ike McCaslin must conquer his fear, his instinct to preserve his separate self from obliteration by submitting to the wholeness represented by the woods. He can completely define himself only in terms of the integrated life force represented by the wilderness and more specifically symbolized by the bear and, later, by the giant rattlesnake.

Ike's faith is justified. Immediately after he has seen the bear, he knows where he is. He has offered his life to the woods, and the woods have given it back to him. Although earlier his spiritual father, Sam Fathers, has anointed him with the blood of his first kill and has shown him the ghostly buck that is the living spirit of wild creatures, Ike's true initiation comes with—to use a Faulknerian term—his self-abnegation. Only after losing his way can he know what Sam has been trying to teach him: that all things are one, all creatures are interdependent, and all are subservient to a greater force that reigns over the universe. To put this in terms at once simpler and more complex: whoever would find his life must lose it. Or be willing to.

This is part of what stories about hunting have taught us, but those I have mentioned were written two generations ago, and the subject no longer flourishes among literary practitioners. When *Modern Fiction Studies* invited submissions for a special issue on sports fiction (Spring, 1987), the editors received many manuscripts, but none on blood sports. Represented among the fourteen essays chosen for publication were swimming, track, boxing, football, and other, less-well-known sports; six of the pieces were about baseball, which suggests that among novelists and critics at least, baseball continues to be the great American pastime. I do not know why baseball has such a strong hold on the public imagination, but one reason may be that it mimics ritual in its superstitions and in the attention that it pays to itself.

Perhaps football and basketball players carry as many rabbits' feet as baseball players, but having no pockets in their uniforms, they cannot carry them onto the field or the court. Of more importance, baseball moves at a slow pace and exposes the participants to much scrutiny. The man at bat pulls his hat brim and spits tobacco juice; the pitcher paces the mound and lifts the resin bag—each according to his own style. For any player to spit or dust his fingers in an unaccustomed way would be to tempt fate, a belief reinforced by the fact that tobacco and bag are traditions of the game. Followers of baseball are asked to appeal to their own gods, particularly during the seventh-inning stretch, an intermission taken at an odd time except that seven is a lucky number, and never to mention that a no-hitter is in progress during the late innings.

Devotees of all sports keep records and write history, but for no other game has the history been so often repeated or so fully documented or have so many different records been kept. There are records for rookies and records for veterans, records for the regular season and for the playoffs and for the World Series. There are records for every position and for every category of play, offensive or defensive, and for aspects of the game so obscure you would think no one would remember to record the facts, but somebody does. This endless keeping of statistics and remembrance of the past lead always inward: each new detail sharpens the focus of attention on the game itself as an enclosed entity, appealing to nothing beyond its own rules and traditions, significant only in terms of its own self-created system.

The disadvantages inherent in the literature of games was well known in the modern period. We used to say that literature was a moral art. The dramatic development of fiction was constructed on the actions of free human beings who chose to do well or ill, a product of the writer's sense that he was reflecting a fallen world with imperfect people in it. Individual moral choices had consequences in the community and appealed, though often subtly, to permanent and objective standards of good and evil. Indeed, until quite recently, the idea of a deity who oversaw the affairs of humankind was usually part of the writer's equipment. Hamlet, who is called to heal the body politic, is diverted by his unchristian application of a Christian principle when he delays killing the king. Gabriel Conroy may be as indifferent to his religion as he is to his native land, but his final epiphany is prepared for and framed by religious discussion and imagery down to the cruciform tops of the spiked fence that stand above the snow.

It would be unfair to say that games are played in a moral vacuum. Certainly baseball players are as sinful as the rest of us, and a game of baseball does offer occasions for sin. On the field and in the dugout, players indulge their emotions: they are gripped with anger, envy, even despair. Traditionally they speak discourteously to each other and to the umpires, and in their worst moments they throw balls and bats at each other and spike each other and fight. Still, the game is the game and it is only that. As long as all are doing their best, as most of the time they are, individual actions and the outcome of the game are matters of skill, not of moral choice. Doubtless many appeals to heaven are made on the mound and at the plate. I once knew a priest who prayed daily in his sacristy for the New York Mets. But these are petitions of individual desire, like a child putting in his bid for a Hershey bar.

Writers of the modern period knew this. For the hero to hit the home run or to strike out the slugger, thus winning the game, was the stuff of juvenile fiction. The athletic feat was embellished by the presence of bad sports, who would cheat if they could, but given the openness of baseball as compared with, say, football—who knows what goes on at the bottom of the pile?—it is hard to cheat. If no one cheats, the drama has no meaning, no matter how exciting the game. A strike-out or a home run becomes a moral act only if one or more of the participants is not doing his best. If a player wants to do what he is supposed to do and fails to do it, we might advise him to find another profession, but he has no moral turpitude to confess. This was one approach modern writers took to baseball. Think of Bernard Malamud's *The Natural* or of stories such as "Jaimie" by J. F. Powers, in which the hometown pitcher deliberately loses the game.

Malamud tries to make more than a mere narrative out of his classic baseball tale. He leads us to see that Roy Hobbs wants to be a star for the wrong reason: out of vanity rather than out of a desire to bring joy to the fans. His hitting slump is cured only when he tries to hit a home run to help a critically ill child. He loves the wrong girl twice: at the beginning of the novel, when Harriet responds to his affection by shooting him, and later, when his infatuation with Memo leads him to accept the judge's bribe to perform poorly in the playoff game. His great hunger for food, which remains unappeased even after he has eaten his way into the hospital, is symbolic of a spiritual hunger that he cannot define. The lake in which he and Iris swim, the mist through which he and

Memo drive, the destruction of his new Mercedes after he has revealed his desire to be the best player who ever lived are symbols too blatant to be overlooked. Some of these scenes seem not to be fully integrated into the novel; some of the symbols may be too obvious. But Malamud's fictional instincts were absolutely right. His story about a game can become significant only when the moral limitations of the game are transcended.

Another, more recently developed way of using baseball in fiction is to deal with its peripheral, perhaps I should say epiphenomenal, aspects: the efforts of not quite sufficiently talented players to get to the big leagues; the domestic disruptions caused by the conditions under which players live—the poverty of those in the minor leagues, the opportunities for infidelity available to the most successful; and the inner struggle of those whose devotion to baseball is tested by conflicting desires. All these themes are found in the more conventional stories of W. P. Kinsella. In "The Baseball Spur" everybody knows that Stan, who is past thirty but still hoping, will never be a big league ballplayer; the climax comes when, by committing a minor act of violence, Stan admits that he too knows. In "Barefoot and Pregnant in Des Moines," the money that Dude Atchison earns as a successful player causes division between him and his wife and prompts his coming unfaithfulness to her. In "Driving Toward the Moon," Johnny abandons his rookie league team and his dream of being a star and drives off into the night with the woman he loves.

So far, as I have tried to state it, the difference between the fiction of blood sports and that of baseball is significant but not absolute. The rituals of hunting carry their transcendent meanings; narratives about baseball must be endowed by their authors with spiritual imagery drawn from outside the game. But all our documents, at least in form and spirit, have been taken from the modern period, a time when remnants of

Judeo-Christian values could still penetrate the artistic world. Now in some postmodern works the game itself has become the reality and therefore the metaphor that interprets life. This development is intimately connected with recent criticism. For example, Don De Lillo's *End Zone* appears to solicit the attention of deconstructionists: it asks to be dealt with as a "text." But De Lillo writes of football. More germane to this discussion is Robert Coover's *The Universal Baseball Association, Inc., J. Henry Waugh, Prop.*

In Coover's novel the focus is not on the game itself, but on a game based on a game, an imagined system one step removed from the real. Waugh organizes his own league, creates his own teams, and invents players, managers, umpires, owners, and a commissioner. He makes schedules, scores each game, keeps records, all for teams and players who exist only in his mind. Increasingly, for Waugh the created game becomes more real than the real game and more authentic to him than his own quotidian life. His devotion to the system he has devised leads him to destroy it by violating the rules he himself has codified. When as a result of a roll of the dice one of his favorite players is hit by a pitched ball and killed, Waugh abandons his posture of unbiased observer. He begins to manipulate the games, helping his favorite team and ultimately bringing about the death of the offending pitcher.

As is the case with De Lillo's *End Zone*, this parable seems to invite us to deal with it as we wish. Is Waugh simply a man too far caught up in a game, or is Coover, like some other writers—John Barth, for example—writing a book about writing a book? As the creator of a world and the people in it, is Waugh really a novelist who loses self-control at the end and begins to manipulate both event and character? The answer here may not be significant. Whatever Waugh is doing, he is playing a game of baseball or a game of literature. In each case the vision is inward; neither the author nor the characters seek any meaning beyond the pastime itself, the relationships within the game to be sorted out, or the minor puzzle to be solved.

Joyce's familiar gospel maintains that art has replaced religion in the ontological scheme. The artist has become a god, but he must maintain detachment. Perhaps the proper reading of Coover's book is to see Waugh as the artist-god who fails in his mission because he allows himself to become emotionally involved with the world he has created. Or perhaps in Coover's more contemporary judgment, artists should participate in their own creations; they should manipulate their plots and people and thereby become characters in their own works. Either way, unlike the fiction of Gordon and Lytle and Faulkner, as well as that of Malamud and Kinsella, Coover's novel seals out not only the sense of the sacred that earlier theories of art as play saw as the source of ritual, but also the possibility of a teleological view of the human condition. If literature is no more than a game, an inward-looking, self-imposed system, then life is also a game and is therefore meaningless.

It is no wonder that such a literature cannot hold its own against any sort of critical theory. If it appeals to nothing beyond itself and has meaning only in its own context, then any kind of deconstructing of the text or any reading of it according to any arbitrarily chosen system is a logical endeavor. Take the work apart, put it together again, and draw whatever conclusion you desire. The game of criticism assumes hegemony over the game of literature. Exploiting this ascendancy, it attacks, often successfully, the classic works that have shaped Western civilization and helped us to define our human state.

What we have lost—let me repeat it—is a sense of the sacred in literature and in life. Without such a sense we are unable to deal with the mysteries that for our forebears were an aspect of being human. Most of these mysteries—the realm of God and angels and devils, the possibility of invisible forces working in the universe, and, for some, the promise of immortality—we can and do ignore. But death is a mystery of many dimensions that we cannot evade. We try to turn away from it by celebrating physical life, by striving to put an end to disease, by eating what we are told is good for us, by exercising, by raising, individually and corporately, every possible defense against what, in our desacralized state, we can only think of as a step into endless darkness. But so far death has refused to meet us on our own terms. Even as we try to develop our myth of physical immortality, friends and acquaintances betray us by dying and, as often as not, compound the betrayal by doing so out of season.

Death is not only the end of life; it collaborates with other seemingly fortuitous events to create a sense of fate that helps to shape our lives and that remains inscrutable. The young die too soon. The old linger and suffer. The good are taken. The bad are spared. The senselessness of the whole idea of death aside, it is fickle and disorderly in its operation. Better, then, we tell ourselves, not to think of it, since it is the last holdout against our concept of a mechanistic universe and a demystified, desacralized world. Better, then, to see life and the literature that life and society engender as mere games. But when we do this, we are lying to ourselves.

"Be absolute for death," said the duke—Shakespeare's line that Eliot made famous. I agree, but not for the reasons given in *Measure for Measure*: not because life is cruel and oblivion is therefore preferable, but because death must be accommodated, its mystery embraced, if life is to be supportable. To embrace it is to engage the possibility of the sacred and to understand, at least partially, the uses of ritual. If we cannot go this far, we can perhaps at least rescue ourselves from the perception that all our endeavors are simply games, no matter how vigorously we pursue them or how seriously we take them. This would be a step toward recovery of the sacred, and both our literature and our criticism would be better for it. In the meantime, the literature of blood sports waits to be read.

Index

Measure for Measure, 119
Southern Renascence, 20, 27, 31, 47
Southern Review, 38, 39
Spencer, Elizabeth, 47
Stewart, Randall, 36
Styron, William, 12
Sullivan, Jane, 53, 54

Tate, Allen, ix, 3–13, 29, 30, 31, 34,
   35, 36, 39, 106; *The Fathers,* 3–
   13
Taylor, Peter, 14–25; "The Death of
   a Kinsman," 14; "A Friend and
   Protector," 14; "The Long
   Fourth," 18–19; "The Old For-
   est," 14, 17, 25; *The Old Forest,*
   18; "Porte Cochère," 25; "Prom-
   ise of Rain," 25; *A Stand in the
   Mountains,* 14–18; *A Summons
   to Memphis,* 23–25; *A Woman of
   Means,* 20–23
Tocqueville, Alexis de, 29
Tolstoy, Leo, 26, 27
Transcendentalists, 27, 30

Vanderbilt Agrarians, 28, 29, 32
Vanderbilt University, 29, 49
Voegelin, Eric, 34

Warren, Robert Penn, 4, 20, 26, 27,
   29, 31, 34, 35, 106; "Blackberry
   Winter," 4
Waugh, Evelyn, 26, 79–88; *Black
   Mischief,* 80; *Brideshead Re-
   visited,* 79, 81, 82–84, 85, 86–87;
   Decline and Fall, 79; *A Handful
   of Dust,* 79, 80; *Helena,* 84–86;
   The Loved One, 79, 84; *The Or-
   deal of Gilbert Pinfold,* 88; *Put
   Out More Flags,* 80; *Scott King's
   Modern Europe,* 84; *Sword of
   Honor,* 86; *Vile Bodies,* 78, 80;
   Work Suspended, 80
Weaver, Richard, 26–37, 38; "Con-
   temporary Southern Literature,"
   30; *The Ethics of Rhetoric,* 28;
   Ideas Have Consequences, 28;
   "The Southern Tradition," 32
Welty, Eudora, 35, 47; *The Ponder
   Heart,* 36
Williams, Charles, 45
Wittgenstein, Ludwig, 33
Wolfe, Thomas, 31

Yeats, William Butler, 89
Young, Stark, 31
Yourcenar, Marguerite, 85